THE MYSTERIES
OF CREATION

The Genesis Story

Books in print by Rocco A. Errico

Setting A Trap for God: The Aramaic Prayer of Jesus
Let There Be Light: The Seven Keys
And There Was Light
The Mysteries of Creation: The Genesis Story
The Message of Matthew: An Annotated Parallel Aramaic-English Gospel of Matthew
Classical Aramaic – Book 1

Spanish publication

La Antigua Oración Aramea de Jesus: El Padrenuestro

German publications

Acht Einstimmungen auf Gott: Vaterunser
Es Werde Licht

Italian publication

Otto accordi con Dio: il Padre Nostro originario

Books in print by Rocco A. Errico and George M. Lamsa
Aramaic New Testament Series: Volumes 1 – 7

Aramaic Light on the Gospel of Matthew
Aramaic Light on the Gospels of Mark and Luke
Aramaic Light on the Gospel of John
Aramaic Light on the Acts of the Apostles
Aramaic Light on Romans through 2 Corinthians
Aramaic Light on Galatians through Hebrews
Aramaic Light on James through Revelation (Fall 2006)

THE MYSTERIES
OF CREATION

The Genesis Story

Rocco A. Errico

The Noohra Foundation, Inc
Smyrna, Georgia

Fourth Printing July 2006

ISBN: 0-9631292-3-6

CONTENTS

PART TWO: THE CREATION STORY

ACKNOWLEDGMENTS

I am deeply grateful to and appreciative of the following individuals: I especially wish to acknowledge Ms. Jeanne Marie Henigin for the many hours she devoted in entering this manuscript in the computer and for her assistance with continual editorial suggestions. Many thanks to the Vice President of the Noohra Foundation, Rev. Richard L. Hill for his constructive comments.

I also wish to express my thanks to Carol Marshall and Rev. Ann D. Milbourn for their practical input and editorial help. And many thanks to Ms. Nell Clement, Mrs. Betty Keller, Ms. Linetta Izenman, Richard Boal and to all the members of the Noohra Foundation whose continual support has made this work possible.

April 7, 1993

NOTE: The ancient Aramaic symbol which appears on the title page of this book is a scribal abbreviation of the name of God: "*Yah*" for "*Yahweh.*" Near Eastern Assyrian Christian scribes usually placed the "*Yah*" at the beginning of a holy book and on the first page of a sacred writing or manuscript.

ABBREVIATIONS

Gen.	Genesis
Ex.	Exodus
Lev.	Leviticus
Deut.	Deuteronomy
2 Sam.	2 Samuel
1 Ki.	1 Kings
2 Ki.	2 Kings
Job	The book of Job
Ps.	Psalms
Prov.	Proverbs
Isa.	Isaiah
Jer.	Jeremiah
Mt.	Matthew
Rev.	Revelation
B.C.E.	Before the Common Era (B.C.)
C.E.	Common Era (A.D.)

PREFACE

In December of 1978 I wrote a twenty-page booklet on the creation story, Genesis — chapter one, based on the Aramaic Peshitta Text of the Hebrew Bible. The Noohra Foundation published this booklet in January 1979. The immediate response to the publication surprised me.

Letters came pouring into the Foundation's headquarters requesting more in-depth comments on the Genesis creation story. And it is from these many requests that I created an outline for my new book *The Mysteries of Creation: The Genesis Story*. Although I have written this book for general readers, certain terminologies and the format I chose require some explanation before beginning.

TERMINOLOGIES

The Bible depicts and understands the national deity of Israel, *Yahweh,* as a masculine god. Therefore, in keeping with the biblical God-notion, I use the masculine pronoun "He" when referring to God throughout this book. Biblical authors did not have the gender-related problems that we are striving to work out in our century. Nor is the biblical view of women negative, sexist, or depreciating as some believe it to be. Derogatory Greek cultural ideas about women gradually began appearing in modified forms in some Jewish literature after the conquest of Alexander the Great in 333 B.C.E. Hebrew scriptures do not vilify women.

I refrained from using the term "myth" too often because of our downbeat understanding of its meaning. We usually equate the words *fantasy, primitive, falsehood* and *superstition* with the meaning of myth. Or, to put it more simply, we commonly see myth as something totally untrue, a work of fiction. It is unfortunate that we have this perspective of myth, because a good portion of the biblical revelation comes to us written as mythopoeic literature.[1]

Throughout the book I employ the terms "cosmology" and "cosmogony." Although these words retain two distinct definitions, I use them interchangeably and do not make definition distinctions. Usually, "cosmology" deals with the origin and development of the universe while "cosmogony" deals with the origin of the solar system.

However, for our purposes in the biblical studies, "cosmogony" (literally: birth of the cosmos) is a tale or an account of the birth of the cosmos. And "cosmology" in a broader sense is a word (*logia*) or a telling of the universe as a comprehensible and meaningful place. Therefore I use both these words interchangeably in the forthcoming chapters. The Genesis story, chapter one, is a cosmogonic and cosmological mythopoeic narrative.

THE FORMAT

Part One, chapters 1–3, is the introduction. Chapter 1 is an overview of authorship, Near Eastern background, how it became written, dates and the purpose of the creation epic. Chapter 2 is my English translation directly from the ancient (MS. — A.D. 464) Peshitta Text of Gen. 1:1–31 and 2:1–3. I have included both Eastern Estrangela Aramaic characters and Western Aramaic consonants (usually called Hebrew letters).

---

[1]See Chapter 1, p. 18, footnote 26 "Mythopoeism."

Chapter 3 is a blend of religious biblical philosophy, modern science (quantum physics), and Aramaic/Hebrew explanations of the names of God. This chapter is based directly on questions that I often receive during my lectures on the creation narrative: "Does God exist?" "What proof is there of God's existence?" "What is God?" "What is the early history of God?" and so forth. Although I discuss some of these questions, most of them would not concern the author of the creation epic. His world and way of thinking were totally different from our modern age and mode of thought.

Part Two, chapters 4-7, is the Creation Story. Chapter 4 probes the meaning of the first two verses in Genesis One. Chapter 5 takes the reader from verse three through verse twenty-five which is the creation process. Chapter 6 explores the idea of humankind and its meaning as the image and likeness of God. Chapter 7 examines Gen. 2:1-3 and summarizes the story of creation.

A FINAL WORD

This work is not a verse-by-verse commentary on the first chapter of Genesis. Nor is this approach a religious, dogmatic one. It does not represent any particular Christian or denominational, theological belief system.

My desire is to help clarify many misunderstandings we may have about the creation story. It is not my intention to coerce, convince or convert anyone to any particular idea. This material is a presentation of my perennial research of Near Eastern Semitic thought and languages of the Bible, which continue to have tremendous influence in our Western society. May your journey into *The Mysteries of Creation: The Genesis Story* be an inspiring, encouraging, and meaningful one.

PART ONE

Introduction

Genesis is not intended to teach 20th century man astronomy, geology and biology, let alone astrophysics or biogenetics.

——————— Robert Gordis

Chapter 1

AN OVERVIEW

THE THEME OF CREATION

Genesis 1:1–2:3,[1] the Hebrew creation narrative, is an ancient prose poem masterpiece. It is a literary depiction and not a literal description of creation. The Semitic author pens a poetically moving scene of the creator, the heavens, the earth and all sentient beings.

The creation narrative presents two basic realizations for the modern reader: (1) that behind the material appearance of the universe is a sacred Intelligence *elohim*[2] and (2) that all creation is a meaningful representation of the creative acts of *elohim*. The author declares the primary objective in the opening phrase "In the beginning God created the heavens and the earth." It is reiterated in the brief and direct phrases "God created," "God exclaimed," "God named," "God separated," "God made," "God blessed," and "God rested." *Elohim* is above and beyond all matter, Creator of the universe, transcendent Being, and Lord over space and time.

---

[1]Many scholars propose that the creation account ends with the first half of the fourth verse of Chapter Two, numbering it as 2:4a. According to these scholars the creation story is: Gen. 1–2:4a. There are also other experts who think that 2:4a is a transitional phrase that does not belong with the cosmogonic narrative.

[2]The Hebrew term for God or a deity is *elohim* See Chapter 4, subheading "*elohim*-God." In Aramaic it is *alaha*. There are no capital letters in Aramaic and Hebrew.

1

The poetic writer presents the reader with a reverent mystery of creation and not an explanation of the cosmos. In essence the narrative says: Here is creative Intelligence at work. Here is an idea of the origin of your viable cosmos, your planet called Earth, and all life.

In the biblical setting, Gen. 1:1–2:3 functions primarily as a precursor to Genesis' thematic scheme: God's involvement in and with the history of humankind and, in particular, with Israel. The first eleven chapters of Genesis serve as a prologue[3] to the narratives of the Hebrew patriarchs, which begin in the twelfth chapter.

THE TITLE

Bresheeth, "In-the-beginning," is the original Hebrew title of the book of Genesis. It is the initial Semitic word of the first verse that opens the book of Genesis and the creation drama. It was a common and universal practice in the ancient Near East to name a manuscript with the word or words that opened the scroll or book. The Peshitta[4] version of the Hebrew Bible

---

[3]Gen. 1–11 is commonly referred to as "primeval history"; but the term "history" can be misleading. The preferred term is "Primeval Cycle."

[4]The Peshitta is the official text of the Bible among Aramaic-speaking Christian lands. In the Near East and India, Christians venerate the Peshitta Bible, Assyrians and Chaldeans, Catholics and non-Catholics. Its originality and authority are upheld by all ancient churches of the East. *Peshitta* means "simple," "pure," "original," or, as applied to the text, "current." As a participle, *peshitta* means "spread out," "not involved, "simplex not duplex," or, again applied to a text, "explicit," "direct," "simple and easy to understand." The Peshitta version is a direct translation from Hebrew. The work was probably done a book at a time, some books by Jews and others by Christians beginning in the first century C.E. and terminating in the third

employs the Aramaic word *breetha* — "The Creation" as the title instead of *bresheeth*. However, Genesis is the name with which most are familiar.

Genesis — "Origin" — comes from the Greek translation of Gen. 2:4a, which says, "This is the book of the origins (*geneseos*) of heaven and earth." The Greek Codex Alexandrinus (5th century C.E.), now in the British Museum, carries the title Genesis Kosmou — "The Origin of the Universe." Genesis informs the reader about origins: the origin of the universe, humankind, Israel, and their relationship to God.

BACKGROUND

Biblical authorities tell us that other Hebrew creation poems and traditions existed in Israel in ancient times. This fact is well attested. For instance, Job 38:4–7 and Isa. 40:12, 21–22, contain remnants and allusions to these earlier creation epics. There are also various scriptural passages alluding to a common primitive tradition which taught that God had to subdue chaotic watery forces.[5] Aramaic names for these legendary forces or creatures are: *yama*, "sea"; *nahra*, "river"; *leviathan*, "the coiled one"; *tanneena*, "dragon." Biblical poets, prophets, and narrators wrote about these legendary beings in the exclusive language of poetry and metaphor.[6] However, in

---

century C.E. However, the date, place, and by whom are conjectural.

[5]See Bernard F. Batto, *Slaying the Dragon: Mythmaking in the Biblical Tradition.* Note that full biographic details appear in the Bibliography unless otherwise cited.

[6]Ps. 74:12–17 and Isa. 51:9–11. See also Jon D. Levenson, *Creation and the Persistence of Evil: The Jewish Drama of Divine Omnipotence.*

the Genesis creation account, the writer sees these forces as natural phenomena created by God.

Within the last century, research into ancient civilizations of the Near East, their languages, and their voluminous body of literature has helped clarify our understanding of Israel's creation story.[7] Ongoing research continues to give us a better grasp of the subtle use of Semitic idioms and symbols. It has also extended our perception of prevailing cosmological notions and motifs of that time.

We can best perceive this genre of creation literature by considering the early Mesopotamian setting in which it was born. If we persist in understanding the biblical creation poem literally, we blur its profound message. The idioms and symbols found in the text represent ideas and meaningful interpretations of our world. Again, if we interpret these metaphors and symbols as reality, we misconstrue the intent and purpose of the creation story. For instance, the number of days for creation was six and one day for rest makes a total of seven days. The number seven is employed by the author as a symbol. It represents perfection and completion. Modern thinkers usually discount the creation story because of a literal seven-day interpretation. The narrator did not realize that this would pose a problem for intellectual minds of the 20th century.

THE NUMBER SEVEN

Near Eastern Semitic people believe that numbers have a meaning greater than just their numerical value. They hold

---

[7]See James B. Pritchard, Ed., *Ancient Near Eastern Texts: Relating to the Old Testament*, third edition with supplement.

that the number seven is the most sacred of all numbers. Yet it is not uncommon for this number to be a part of their daily customs and manners. For example, according to an old eastern custom, when a king sat in council he generally had six ministers of state seated with him, three on his right and three on his left. This seating arrangement of the king and his six ministers, seven all together, formed a quorum.

Biblical authors extensively used the sacred number seven in their writings. The first chapter of Genesis abounds in the subtle use of the number seven (i.e., the heptadic principle). Gen. 1:1, in its original Semitic language, contains seven words; the second verse contains fourteen words (2 x 7); the narrative itself contains seven literary units consisting of six creation days and the final day of rest.

The meticulous scholar Umberto Cassuto delved deeply into the creation text and showed that the number seven could hardly be limited just to the days of creation. He tells us that three major nouns used throughout the text, i.e., "God," "heaven" and "earth" are used in multiples of seven. "God" occurs thirty-five times (7 x 5); "heaven" and "earth" occur twenty-one times each (7 x 3). His research is so exhaustive that I will mention only a few of his examples of the heptadic principle. The author uses the term "water" seven times in paragraphs two and three. The expression "that it was beautiful" (Hebrew: "that it was good") appears seven times. The paragraph which relates to the seventh day consists of thirty-five words (7 x 5), twenty-one of which form three sentences of seven words, each of which makes use of the term "the seventh day."[8]

One more example of the biblical heptadic principle is The Revelation, the last book of the New Testament. The literary design of this prophetic book is a sevenfold structure. There are seven visions contained within the body of The Revelation, and each individual vision is in seven parts. It is replete with specialized utilization of seven i.e., seven churches, angels (messengers) admonitions, lampstands, seals, trumpets, bowls, and so forth.

Some researchers claim that adoption of the number seven may have originated from pristine astronomy. Seven planets were known to the ancients, i.e., Sun, Moon, Mercury, Venus, Mars, Jupiter, and Saturn. The Jewish and Muhammad-an calendars are based upon the phases of the moon, and their months have twenty-eight days. Seven is a quarterly division of this unit. Remember, in the Near East seven signifies the basic idea of design, completion, and perfection. We have learned from historical research that the ancient Mesopotamian world employed the heptadic principle as a common literary device.

THE BIBLE AND TORAH

The term "Bible" was not used in the old Semitic languages of Aramaic and Hebrew. Our English word bible is derived from the Greek word *biblia* meaning "books." The original descriptive term for the Bible was "scriptures" or "the

---

[8]For more examples of the authorial usage of the number seven see U. Cassuto, *Commentary on the Book of Genesis, Part One: From Adam to Noah*, pp. 12–15.

writings." When the Greek word for "scriptures" was translated into Latin, the word *biblia* was substituted to denote a collection or library of books. This collection was also known as "The Sacred Writings."

The creation story is part of the *torah*. Although the Semitic word *torah* has a deeper meaning, it is usually translated as the "Law." This translation came about when the scribes rendered the word *torah* in the Greek language as *nomos,* which strictly means "Law." However, *torah* does refer to the laws of Moses, which are recorded in the books of Exodus, Leviticus, Numbers, and Deuteronomy. Nonetheless, the Greek word *nomos* fails to convey the full import of this Semitic Hebrew term.

The word *torah* has the significance of doctrine and instruction and usually refers to the first five books of Hebrew scriptures: Genesis through Deuteronomy. Contemporary Jewish authorities refer to all Hebrew Scriptures under the acronym *Tanakh,* which is derived from dividing Holy Scripture into three sections: *torah* = *T* (Gen. to Deut.), *nevi'im* = *N* (Prophets), and the *kithuvim* = *K* (Writings). Thus the acronym *TNKH — Tanakh.*

The name given to the Hebrew scriptures in Aramaic, the common and predominant language of Palestine in the first century C.E., is *oretha*, meaning "teaching" and "enlightenment." It is equivalent to *torah.* Aramaic and Hebrew lexicons explain that both words are derived from the Semitic root *yrh* and mean to "guide," "direct," "teach," and "instruct." Thus Holy Scripture is a book of guidance, instruction, and teaching intended to enlighten humankind. It is a record of Hebrew law, drama, sacred history, poetry, philosophy, psychology, and religion.

However, sacred scripture may be viewed from yet another perspective. Spiritual principles are revealed, discerned

7

and understood through the spiritual capacity of the mind, i.e., through higher consciousness or awareness. In other words, the Bible uncovers intangible spiritual matters that pertain and speak to the heart and soul of its readers. Thus we may also think of the Holy Text as a book of the light of the soul, a metaphysical history of transcending consciousness — that is, a history which tells the story of human consciousness constantly rising above culture, environments, difficult situations, and trying events, including self-imposed limitations. It tells of a nation that encountered something beyond the ordinary.

Undoubtedly, biblical folklore was originally spoken, not written. People passed on these stories by word of mouth and from one eager heart to another. Even during New Testament times the Semitic Palestinian world remained very much an oral culture. Jeremiah, the prophet, predicted the day when the Lord (*yahweh*) would write the *torah* on the hearts of the people and not just on clay tablets. "Now this is the agreement that I shall make with the family of Israel, after those days, says the Lord: I will put my *torah* in the midst of them and I will write it on their hearts; and I will be their God and they shall be my people."[9]

In ancient days, Hebrew religion and tradition were tribal-family affairs. We can use our imagination and picture the Semitic environment of those early times. Visualize biblical narratives told to sons by fathers and to daughters by mothers in their homes or around the open fire under the twinkling firmament. Presumably, all religious and nationalistic stories were spoken and taught in a special ambience — an atmosphere created within and by the family circle or by the elders of the clans.

---

[9]Jer. 31:33, Aramaic Peshitta Text, Errico translation.

DATING THE CREATION STORY

When was the Hebrew text of creation composed and under what circumstances was it written? Is it possible to know the conditions that influenced and prompted the author to pen his account of creation?

Biblical experts plausibly date the text of the creation narrative around the 6th century, B.C.E.[10] and believe the author wrote it for the exiled Jews in Chaldea (Babylon). According to these authorities, the banished Hebrews were to know that the gods of Chaldea (Babylon) had not won a decisive victory over the God of Israel and His people. The mighty Deity of the Hebrews was not only their God but, according to the creation writing, He alone was the Creator. There were no other deities present when *elohim* created heaven and earth. No divinity existed in anything that God created. Genesis 1 makes it clear that heaven itself did not house any god or gods. All these things were God's creative acts. He was sovereign Lord of all.

Whatever the authentic background may have been, the detailed issue of its historical setting will not be explored in this

---

[10]It is important to note that several scholars do not agree with this late date for the Genesis cosmogony and in fact call into question any late dating of the Priestly writings of the Torah. Furthermore, others have observed that even if Genesis 1–2:3 was written during the Exile, this creation story originates from an earlier time in Israel's history. See G. von Rad, *Old Testament Theology*, tr. D. M. G. Stalker, 2 vols., 1962–1965. Hebrew scriptures were written and shaped during a period of a thousand years. The Bible's earliest poems were probably composed and penned 1200–1000 B.C.E. The books that make up the present Hebrew Bible, known as the *canon*, were chosen around the period of the conquest of Alexander the Great. The late additions to the biblical canon were *Ecclesiastes* and most probably *The Song of Solomon*.

book. My intention is to yield essential insight and understanding for modern readers of the creation text. I will focus on a few necessary historical facts for clarification only. Also, I wish to familiarize the readers with ancient Semitic ideas.

AUTHORSHIP

German scholars in the latter part of the last century began proposing that the first five books of the Bible (Genesis, Exodus, Leviticus, Numbers, and Deuteronomy) emerged from four distinct primitive traditions. These sources of tradition are known as "J" — Yahwist; "E" — Elohist; "P" — Priestly and "D" — author of Deuteronomy. There is also another known as "R" — the Redactor[11] of the final text of all five books. The book of Genesis is composed of three traditions — "J," "E," and "P" — and, of course, there is the hand of the Redactor.

This German proposal, known as the "Documentary Hypothesis," had won over most of biblical authorities by 1875. The hypothesis radically changed the method in which biblical interpretation was practiced. However, since the turn of the 20th century, notable scholars have vehemently challenged this theory.[12] Their challenge rests not on the basis of religious belief alone, but on arguments that the documentarians

---

[11]A German word meaning "editor."

[12]Such scholars as Benno Jacob, Umberto Cassuto, Yehezkel Kaufmann, J. Dahse, W. Moller (who was later joined by P. Volz and W. Rudolph). For an overview of the latest discussion of the "Documentary Hypothesis" see Claus Westermann, *Genesis 1–11: An Introduction*, pp. 76–91: "Pentateuchal Research": (1) Toward a Revision of the Documentary Hypothesis and (2) The Criteria for Source Division. Also: Joseph Blenkinsopp, *The Pentateuch*, pp. 1–30: "Two Centuries of Pentateuchal Scholarship."

themselves posit.[13] At least six basic objections to this hypothesis exist. The objectors claim that these German scholars misunderstood classical Hebrew and did not possess sufficient knowledge of ancient Semitic thinking to create an accurate hypothesis.

According to the "Documentary Hypothesis," Gen. 1:1 through 2:4a was alleged to have been written by "P" — Priestly School. Nevertheless, there are other scholars who contend that only one author wrote the book of Genesis.[14] In addition, there are those authorities who hold: (1) that Moses was responsible for the basic tradition of the first five books, and (2) that he wrote the laws for his people while they were in the desert. No matter who the author or authors may have been, all biblical writings were edited by Hebrew scribes before those writings were ever accepted as sacred canon.

Since it is not my intention to present a critical, historical analysis of Genesis, the question of authorship will not be developed further in this volume. My purpose here is to offer some historical facts, findings, and opinions, and not to argue authorship.[15]

---

[13]See U. Cassuto, *The Documentary Hypothesis: Eight Lectures,* tr. Israel Abrahams.

[14]For a very interesting theory and scholarly work on the idea of "one author," see Yehuda T. Radday and Haim Shore, *Genesis: An Authorship Study*.

[15]It is for the reader to decide the issue of authorship. Presently, I think that the creation account was probably the work of a priest-prophet (like Ezekiel). He received and reshaped ancient widespread creation motifs and traditions. And, undoubtedly, earlier Israelite creation poems guided him.

STYLE OF WRITING

The first chapter of the creation epic is written in a form typical of the Near East.[16] Its terse statements are presented in prose form with mystical and imaginative overtones. This style of writing is natural to the Near Eastern poetic heart and soul. Repetitious phrases flow rhythmically, painting a dramatic scene of divine order in the midst of chaos. The creation process peaks with humankind and closes with the beauty and tranquility of all creation. The narrator declares that God felt deep satisfaction when His dynamic creative acts were completed. God established universal order through creative commands and a series of checks and balances. He "separated the light from the darkness." He created a firmament to "divide the waters from the waters," and gathered the waters in "one place." *Elohim* created lights in the heavens for the separation of day and night. These lights were for signs, seasons, days, and years. One receives the impression from reading the account that a cosmic contentment was everywhere present when God finished His work. In Gen. 1:31, he says to the reader: "Then God observed everything that He had made and behold it was exceedingly beautiful. Now it was evening, then it was morning, day six."[17]

---

[16]Experts hold that the language and style of biblical poetry continue the traditions of ancient Canaan. See M. P. O'Connor, *Hebrew Verse Structure*, and Adele Berlin, *The Dynamics of Biblical Parallelism*.

[17]Aramaic Peshitta Text, Errico translation, Gen. 1:31. For the complete translation of the first chapter of Genesis, see Chapter 2, "The Aramaic Peshitta Text English Translation of Genesis 1:1–2:3."

The Eastern poet who set down the creation composition must have been a sensitive individual who wrote from the perspective of his soul. He saw and felt the aliveness of the earth and the viability and oneness of all life. He perceived the holiness of the earth and the sacredness of the human family and all living creatures. To impart this perception he employed a nonliteral poetic style of writing.

THE ANCIENT NEAR EAST

We as readers of the biblical cosmogony need to be drawn into the Near Eastern atmosphere and intent of the narrator. Once this is established, we can then capture the idea of the creation story. This is best accomplished by not imposing upon the text our modern scientific forms of rationalization. Nor should we allow our particular religious faith to impinge upon this ancient writing. Neither should we look for proofs within the narrative for the existence of God. The biblical writer is not concerned with empirical data to prove God's existence. It is never questioned at all.

Israel and all nations of the ancient Near East believed that a god, gods, or goddesses had created their world and all living creatures. A biblical commentator informs us:

> . . . there was no viable alternative. There was no understanding of the existence of humanity or of the world which was not based on the conviction of creation. If we want to understand the Old Testament when it talks about creator and creation, then we should not associate it with or subject it to a concept of faith that presumes such an alternative.[18]

---

[18]Claus Westermann, *Genesis 1-11: A Commentary,* pp. 42–43.

The author narrates the creative process in the familiar cosmological terms and motifs of the times. He simply says that God spoke the commanding prophetic word "and that is how it happened." In those days people believed that the creation of the gods, goddesses, and the world occurred in at least one of four major ways: (1) through birth (sexual activity), (2) through the spoken word, (3) through struggle, and (4) through making or forming.[19] Thus, creating through utterance was an ancient means of describing the creative process. However, this does not imply that the *torah* creation composition was necessarily dependent upon any other ancient cosmogonic texts, be they Egyptian, Chaldean, or Canaanite.

What the writer reveals about creation is his spiritual realization based on Near Eastern motifs of great antiquity. The text challenges the reader to join with the spirit and imagination of the narrator. An understanding of the author's Semitic intellectual temperament and a comprehensive overview of his cultural-religious world is required to apprehend the creation story more clearly. This kind of realization will move the reader beyond the words and symbolic descriptions contained in the text to richer and deeper levels of understanding.

THE BABYLONIAN COSMOGONY

Certain biblical historians report that segments of the creation account were probably based on ancient cosmological traditions of the Sumerians, Assyrians, Chaldeans, Egyptians and, in particular, on the so-called Babylonian cosmogony

---

[19]The above should not be taken as a comprehensive account of cosmogonic beginnings. Legendary epics vary considerably.

known as *Enuma Elish,* "When on High." After a comprehensive study of this Mesopotamian version of cosmic origins (*Enuma Elish*), these authorities say that not only is there a striking similarity between it and the Hebrew account, but the order of events is identical. They believe this fact to be most significant and not just coincidental. What follows is a comparison of the two texts:

GENESIS	ENUMA ELISH
1) Chaos; darkness covering deep	1) Primeval chaos; the Ti'amat (the sea) enveloped in darkness
2) Light created	2) Light from the gods
3) Creation of firmament	3) Firmament
4) Creation of dry land	4) Dry land
5) Creation of luminaries	5) Luminaries
6) Creation of man	6) Man
7) God rests and hallows the seventh day	7) The gods rest and are festive[20]

However, other scholars contend that the biblical writer reflected the known, general cosmological ideas[21] and knowledge of his era. In other words, the author did not base his writing on any non-Israelite cosmologies, but on earlier Israelite creation compositions. Still others profess that the Genesis creation account is a polemic against the gods and beliefs of that epoch.

---

[20]E. A. Speiser, *Genesis: A New Translation with Introduction and Commentary,* pp. 9–10.

[21]See above subheading "The Ancient Near East."

15

Regardless, even if the biblical writer borrowed from other ancient Near Eastern traditions, his writings were peculiarly characteristic of the Hebrew setting. Also, some of his conclusions were different from those expressed in non-Israelite texts. For instance, he sees all nature and its dynamic energies not as divinities but as natural forces created by and under the sovereignty of *elohim*. Furthermore, the *torah* creation account tells nothing of the origin of the creator, which is the deity *elohim*. But most of the other Near Eastern creation accounts tell of the births of the gods and goddesses.[22] There are various differences between Hebrew traditions and the prevailing myths of the times. On the other hand, there are also many similarities and parallels.[23]

Many early cosmogonic sagas portrayed humanity in the image of their gods.[24] It is an accepted and well-grounded scholarly opinion that the biblical idea of humanity created in "the image and likeness of God" is derived from Sumerian tradition. However, the biblical setting differs from the Sumerian context. It is only the motif that is the same.

What the Genesis account implies by portraying a human being as the very image and likeness of God is that humans are children of God. This relationship is vital, and humanity needs to understand its depths. The implication is wonderful! Would that the human family carried it out!

---

[22]Any account or story of the origins of gods and goddesses is referred to as a "theogony."

[23]My focus is not a comparative analysis of biblical texts or extra-biblical traditions. I refer you to the Bibliography.

[24]See Claus Westermann, *Genesis: An Introduction*, "(b) The Formation of Humanity," pp. 35–38.

It is a basic biblical truth that all races come from a common source. In other words, it is a spiritual, that is, a transcendental ethnic source which unites humankind. What this simply means is that we may interact with spiritual forces that are inherent within every individual. All humans are to be treated respectfully despite birth or social status. The sages understood that knowing one's spiritual source would promote social harmony. They further understood that no person could claim unique ancestry as a pretext for asserting superiority over others.

To this very day Easterners believe that every child born in this world is God's offspring, i.e., God's life reproducing itself in the life of a human being. To the ancient Near Eastern biblical writer, reproduction in all the worlds of life was profoundly sacred and precious. In retelling the creation story, individuals could find meaning for their existence. And not only for their particular existence, but also for the existence of the entire cosmos and all races of the earth.

SUMMARY

Our present scientific knowledge of the universe may make the biblical creation account (Gen. 1–2:3) appear to the reader as crude, naive, and extremely primitive. In the chapters to come we will take a closer look at the "primitive" presentation of creation. Nonetheless, its basic message is one that encourages universal human rights, freedom, and dignity.

Let us also understand that each Near Eastern cosmological tradition that was prevalent among the nations and clans of the ancient Mediterranean world represented a way in which they could relate to themselves and to their social world. In fact, the many myths of the gods and goddesses played a major part in helping them understand the culturally distinctive social roles of the sexes.[25]

It is my conviction that before composing the creation account the mythopoeic[26] author clearly perceived the importance of what he was about to do. He rightfully placed the heavens, the earth and the entire human family in its divinely ordered setting. He understood his world and universe as a creation of God. The author further understood *elohim* as the only creator and knew that *elohim* had crowned humankind with dignity as His "image and likeness." This is the biblical backdrop of the simple yet magnificent creation story we are about to read in the forthcoming chapters. So let us begin the story of creation.

---

[25]For an overall view of the Role of Cosmology in Religion, see *The Anchor Bible Dictionary,* vol. 1, pp. 1170–71, "(2) Recent Formulations of the Place of Cosmology in Religion."

[26]"Mythopoeism" derives from two Greek words, *mythos* and *poein.* Bernard F. Batto, Assoc. Prof. of Religion, DePauw University, defines *mythopoeic* as "the process by which new myths are created or old myths are extended to include new dimensions." He further says that the process is a "*conscious* reflected application of older myths and mythic elements to new situations" in contrast to "*preconscious*" or "unreflective statements about reality." B.F. Batto, *Slaying the Dragon: Mythmaking in the Biblical Tradition*, "The Definition of Myth" pp. 4–14.

THE CREATION NARRATIVE

GENESIS 1:1 – 2:3

THE PESHITTA ARAMAIC TEXT
464 A. D. (C.E.)

TRANSLATED BY

ROCCO A. ERRICO

THE ARAMAIC PESHITTA TEXT
ENGLISH TRANSLATION OF
GENESIS 1:1 – 2:3

**In the beginning
God created
the heavens and the earth.**

**Now the earth was chaos,
and darkness was upon the deep.
And the spirit of God hovered compassionately
over the surface of the waters**

**Then God exclaimed:
Let there be light!
And there was light.
Now God saw the light that it was beautiful.
So God separated the light from the darkness.
Then God named the light: Day.
And He named the darkness: Night.
Now it was evening,
then it was morning,
day one.**

Chapter 2

THE ARAMAIC PESHITTA TEXT
OF
GENESIS 1:1 – 2:3

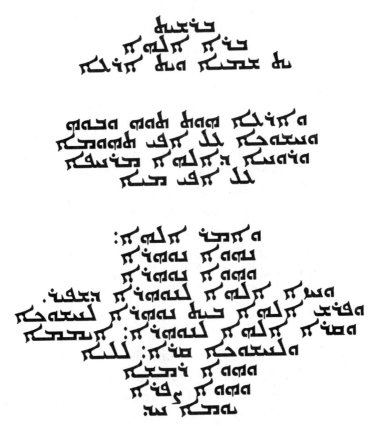

Then God exclaimed:
Let there be a firmament in the midst of the waters,
and let it separate the waters from the waters!
So God made the firmament
and separated the waters that are under the firmament
from the waters that are above the firmament.
And that is how it happened.
Then God named the firmament: Sky.
Now it was evening,
then it was morning,
day two.

Then God exclaimed:
Let the waters that are under the sky
come together into one place,
and let dry land appear!
And that is how it happened.
Then God named the dry land: Earth.
And He named the collection of waters: Seas.
Now God saw that it was beautiful.

Then God exclaimed:
Let the earth sprout vegetation,
the herb-yielding seed according to its nature,
and the fruit tree that bears fruit
that is implanted in itself according to its nature,
upon the earth!
And that is how it happened.
So the earth sprouted vegetation,
the herb-yielding seed according to its nature,

22

ܘܐܡܪ ܐܠܗܐ:
ܢܗܘܐ ܪܩܝܥܐ ܒܡܨܥܬ ܡܝܐ
ܘܢܗܘܐ ܦܪܫ ܒܝܢ ܡܝܐ ܠܡܝܐ
ܘܥܒܕ ܐܠܗܐ ܪܩܝܥܐ
ܘܦܪܫ ܒܝܢ ܡܝܐ ܕܠܬܚܬ ܡܢ ܪܩܝܥܐ
ܘܒܝܢ ܡܝܐ ܕܠܥܠ ܡܢ ܪܩܝܥܐ
ܘܗܘܐ ܗܟܢܐ
ܘܩܪܐ ܐܠܗܐ ܠܪܩܝܥܐ: ܫܡܝܐ
ܘܗܘܐ ܪܡܫܐ
ܘܗܘܐ ܨܦܪܐ
ܝܘܡܐ ܕܬܪܝܢ

ܘܐܡܪ ܐܠܗܐ:
ܢܬܟܢܫܘܢ ܡܝܐ ܕܠܬܚܬ ܡܢ ܫܡܝܐ
ܠܐܬܪܐ ܚܕ:
ܘܬܬܚܙܐ ܝܒܝܫܬܐ
ܘܗܘܐ ܗܟܢܐ
ܘܩܪܐ ܐܠܗܐ ܠܝܒܝܫܬܐ: ܐܪܥܐ
ܘܠܟܢܫܐ ܕܡܝܐ ܩܪܐ: ܝܡܡܐ
ܘܚܙܐ ܐܠܗܐ ܕܫܦܝܪ

ܘܐܡܪ ܐܠܗܐ:
ܬܦܩ ܐܪܥܐ ܬܕܐܐ
ܥܣܒܐ ܕܡܙܕܪܥ ܙܪܥܐ ܠܓܢܣܗ
ܘܐܝܠܢܐ ܕܦܐܪܐ ܕܥܒܕ ܦܐܪܐ
ܕܙܪܥܗ ܒܗ
ܥܠ ܐܪܥܐ
ܘܗܘܐ ܗܟܢܐ
ܘܐܦܩܬ ܐܪܥܐ ܬܕܐܐ
ܥܣܒܐ ܕܡܙܕܪܥ ܙܪܥܐ ܠܓܢܣܗ

and the fruit tree that bears fruit
that is implanted in itself according to its nature.
And God saw that it was beautiful.
Now it was evening,
then it was morning,
day three.

Then God exclaimed:
Let there be lights in the firmament of the sky
to separate the day from the night;
and let them be for signs,
and for seasons, and for days
and for years!
And let them shine in the firmament of the sky
to give light on the earth!
And that is how it happened.
So God made two great lights,
the larger light to rule over the day
and the smaller light to rule over the night
and the stars.
And God entrusted them to the firmament of the sky
to give light on the earth,
and to rule over the day
and over the night
and to separate the light from the darkness.
And God saw that it was beautiful.
Now it was evening,
then it was morning,
day four.

ܘܐܝܠܢܐ ܕܥܒܕ ܦܐܪܐ
ܕܙܪܥܗ ܒܗ ܠܓܢܣܗ
ܘܚܙܐ ܐܠܗܐ ܕܫܦܝܪ
ܘܗܘܐ ܪܡܫܐ
ܘܗܘܐ ܨܦܪܐ
ܝܘܡܐ ܕܬܠܬܐ

ܘܐܡܪ ܐܠܗܐ:
ܢܗܘܘܢ ܢܗܝܪܐ ܒܪܩܝܥܐ ܕܫܡܝܐ
ܠܡܦܪܫ ܒܝܬ ܐܝܡܡܐ ܠܠܠܝܐ
ܘܢܗܘܘܢ ܠܐܬܘܬܐ
ܘܠܙܒܢܐ ܘܠܝܘܡܬܐ
ܘܠܫܢܝܐ
ܘܢܗܘܘܢ ܡܢܗܝܪܝܢ ܒܪܩܝܥܐ ܕܫܡܝܐ
ܠܡܢܗܪܘ ܥܠ ܐܪܥܐ
ܘܗܘܐ ܗܟܢܐ
ܘܥܒܕ ܐܠܗܐ ܬܪܝܢ ܢܗܝܪܐ ܪܘܪܒܐ
ܢܗܝܪܐ ܪܒܐ ܠܫܘܠܛܢܐ ܕܐܝܡܡܐ
ܘܢܗܝܪܐ ܙܥܘܪܐ ܠܫܘܠܛܢܐ ܕܠܠܝܐ
ܘܟܘܟܒܐ
ܘܝܗܒ ܐܢܘܢ ܐܠܗܐ ܒܪܩܝܥܐ ܕܫܡܝܐ
ܠܡܢܗܪܘ ܥܠ ܐܪܥܐ
ܘܠܡܫܠܛ ܒܐܝܡܡܐ
ܘܒܠܠܝܐ
ܘܠܡܦܪܫ ܒܝܬ ܢܘܗܪܐ ܠܚܫܘܟܐ
ܘܚܙܐ ܐܠܗܐ ܕܫܦܝܪ
ܘܗܘܐ ܪܡܫܐ
ܘܗܘܐ ܨܦܪܐ
ܝܘܡܐ ܕܐܪܒܥܐ

Then God exclaimed:
Let the waters be teeming
with swarms of living creatures,
and let the flying creatures fly above the earth
and in the open expanse of the sky!
So God created huge dragons
and all living creatures that swarm
which the waters brought forth according to their kind
and every flying creature according to its kind.
Now God saw that it was beautiful.
Then God blessed them
and said to them:
Be fruitful and increase
and fill the waters of the seas,
and let the flying creatures increase on the earth!
Now it was evening,
then it was morning,
day five.

Then God exclaimed:
Let the earth bring forth living creatures
according to their nature:
animals and reptiles and wild land beasts
according to their nature!
And that is how it happened.
So God made the wild land beasts
according to their nature
and the animals according to their nature
and all the reptiles of the earth
according to their nature.
And God saw that it was beautiful.

26

ܘܐܡܪ ܐܠܗܐ:
ܢܪܚܫܘܢ ܡܝܐ
ܪܚܫܐ ܢܦܫܐ ܚܝܬܐ
ܘܦܪܚܬܐ ܬܦܪܚ ܥܠ ܐܪܥܐ
ܥܠ ܐܦܝ ܪܩܝܥܐ ܕܫܡܝܐ
ܘܒܪܐ ܐܠܗܐ ܬܢܝܢܐ ܪܘܪܒܐ
ܘܟܠ ܢܦܫܐ ܚܝܬܐ ܕܪܚܫܐ
ܕܐܪܚܫܘ ܡܝܐ ܠܓܢܣܗܘܢ
ܘܟܠ ܦܪܚܬܐ ܕܓܦܐ ܠܓܢܣܗ̇
ܘܚܙܐ ܐܠܗܐ ܕܫܦܝܪ
ܘܒܪܟ ܐܢܘܢ ܐܠܗܐ
ܘܐܡܪ ܠܗܘܢ
ܦܪܘ ܘܣܓܘ
ܘܡܠܘ ܡܝܐ ܕܒܝܡܡܐ
ܘܦܪܚܬܐ ܬܣܓܐ ܒܐܪܥܐ
ܘܗܘܐ ܪܡܫܐ
ܘܗܘܐ ܨܦܪܐ
ܝܘܡܐ ܕܚܡܫܐ

ܘܐܡܪ ܐܠܗܐ:
ܬܦܩ ܐܪܥܐ ܢܦܫܐ ܚܝܬܐ
ܠܓܢܣܗ̇
ܒܥܝܪܐ ܘܪܚܫܐ ܘܚܝܘܬܐ ܕܐܪܥܐ
ܠܓܢܣܗ̇
ܘܗܘܐ ܗܟܢܐ
ܘܥܒܕ ܐܠܗܐ ܚܝܘܬܐ ܕܐܪܥܐ
ܠܓܢܣܗ̇
ܘܒܥܝܪܐ ܠܓܢܣܗ̇
ܘܟܠܗ ܪܚܫܐ ܕܐܪܥܐ
ܠܓܢܣܗ̇
ܘܚܙܐ ܐܠܗܐ ܕܫܦܝܪ

Then God exclaimed:
Let us make humankind in our image,
as our resemblance!
And they shall rule over the fish of the sea,
and over the flying creatures of the sky,
and over the animals,
and over all the wild land beasts,
and over all the reptiles
that creep on the earth!
So God created humankind
in His image,
in the image of God
He created him,
male and female
He created them.
Then God blessed them
and said to them:
Be fruitful and increase
and fill the earth and master it!
And rule over the fish of the sea
and over the flying creatures of the sky
and over the wild land beasts
and over all the animals that walk on the earth!

Then God said:
Behold I have given you every herb-yielding seed
that is planted upon the surface of the earth,
and every tree that bears fruit-yielding seed;
to you it shall be for food.
And to every animal of the field

ܘܐܡܪ ܐܠܗܐ:
ܢܥܒܕ ܐܢܫܐ ܒܨܠܡܢ
ܐܝܟ ܕܡܘܬܢ
ܘܢܫܠܛܘܢ ܒܢܘܢܝ ܝܡܐ
ܘܒܦܪܚܬܐ ܕܫܡܝܐ
ܘܒܒܥܝܪܐ
ܘܒܟܠܗ ܚܝܘܬܐ ܕܐܪܥܐ
ܘܒܟܠܗ ܪܚܫܐ
ܕܪܚܫ ܥܠ ܐܪܥܐ
ܘܒܪܐ ܐܠܗܐ ܠܐܕܡ
ܒܨܠܡܗ
ܒܨܠܡ ܐܠܗܐ
ܒܪܝܗܝ
ܕܟܪ ܘܢܩܒܐ
ܒܪܐ ܐܢܘܢ
ܘܒܪܟ ܐܢܘܢ ܐܠܗܐ
ܘܐܡܪ ܠܗܘܢ ܐܠܗܐ:
ܦܪܘ ܘܣܓܘ
ܘܡܠܘ ܐܪܥܐ ܘܟܒܘܫܘܗ
ܘܫܠܛܘ ܒܢܘܢܝ ܝܡܐ
ܘܒܦܪܚܬܐ ܕܫܡܝܐ
ܘܒܒܥܝܪܐ
ܘܒܟܠܗ ܚܝܘܬܐ ܕܪܚܫܐ ܥܠ ܐܪܥܐ

ܘܐܡܪ ܐܠܗܐ:
ܗܐ ܝܗܒܬ ܠܟܘܢ ܟܠܗ ܥܣܒܐ ܕܙܪܥܐ
ܕܡܙܕܪܥ ܥܠ ܐܦܝ ܟܠܗ ܐܪܥܐ
ܘܟܠ ܐܝܠܢ ܕܐܝܬ ܒܗ ܦܐܪܐ ܐܝܠܢܐ
ܕܙܪܥܗ ܡܙܕܪܥܐ
ܠܟܘܢ ܢܗܘܐ ܠܡܐܟܘܠܬܐ
ܘܠܟܠܗ ܚܝܘܬܐ ܕܕܒܪܐ

and to all flying creatures of the sky
and to everything that creeps on the earth
that has life [I give]
all tender green herbs for food.
And that is how it happened.

Then God observed everything
that He had made.
And behold:
it was exceedingly beautiful!
Now it was evening,
then it was morning,
day six.

And they were finished,
the heavens and the earth
and all their powers.
Now on the sixth day
God had finished His works
that He had made.
So He rested on the seventh day
from all His works that He had made.
Then God blessed the seventh day
and made it holy
because on that day
He rested from all his works
that He created and made.

ܘܠܟܠܗ ܦܪܚܬܐ ܕܫܡܝܐ
ܘܠܟܠ ܕܪܚܫ ܥܠ ܐܪܥܐ
ܕܐܝܬ ܒܗ ܢܦܫܐ ܚܝܬܐ
ܘܟܠܗ ܝܘܪܩܐ ܕܥܣܒܐ ܠܡܐܟܘܠܬܐ
ܘܗܘܐ ܗܟܢܐ

ܘܚܙܐ ܐܠܗܐ ܟܠ
ܕܥܒܕ
ܘܗܐ
ܛܒ ܫܦܝܪ
ܘܗܘܐ ܪܡܫܐ
ܘܗܘܐ ܨܦܪܐ
ܝܘܡܐ ܕܫܬܐ

ܘܫܠܡܘ ܫܡܝܐ ܘܐܪܥܐ
ܘܟܠܗ ܚܝܠܗܘܢ
ܘܫܠܡ ܐܠܗܐ
ܒܝܘܡܐ ܫܬܝܬܝܐ ܥܒܕܘܗܝ
ܕܥܒܕ
ܘܐܬܬܢܝܚ ܒܝܘܡܐ ܫܒܝܥܝܐ
ܡܢ ܟܠܗܘܢ ܥܒܕܘܗܝ ܕܥܒܕ
ܘܒܪܟ ܐܠܗܐ ܠܝܘܡܐ ܫܒܝܥܝܐ
ܘܩܕܫܗ
ܡܛܠ ܕܒܗ
ܐܬܬܢܝܚ ܡܢ ܟܠܗܘܢ ܥܒܕܘܗܝ
ܕܒܪܐ ܐܠܗܐ ܠܡܥܒܕ

❖ ❖ ❖

THE ARAMAIC PESHITTA TEXT
GENESIS 1:1 – 2:3
IN
WESTERN ARAMAIC

בְּרֵשִׁית
בְּרָא אֱלָהָא
יָת שְׁמַיָא וְיָת אַרְעָא

וְאַרְעָא הֲוָת תּוֹה וּבוֹה
וַחֲשׁוֹכָא עַל אַפֵּי תְהוֹמָא
וְרוּחָא דֵּאלָהָא מְרַחְפָא
עַל אַפֵּי מַיָא

וַאֲמַר אֱלָהָא:
נֶהְוֵא נוּהְרָא
וַהֲוָא נוּהְרָא
וַחֲזָא אֱלָהָא לְנוּהְרָא דְּשַׁפִּירָא.
וּפְרַשׁ אֱלָהָא בֵּית נוּהְרָא לַחֲשׁוֹכָא
וּקְרָא אֱלָהָא לְנוּהְרָא: אִימָמָא
וְלַחֲשׁוֹכָא קְרָא: לֵלְיָא
וַהֲוָא רַמְשָׁא
וַהֲוָא צַפְרָא
יוֹמָא חַד

32

ואמר אלהא:
נהוא רקיעא במצעת מיא
ונהוא פרש בית מיא למיא
ועבד אלהא רקיעא
ופרש בית מיא דלתחת מן רקיעא
ובית מיא דלעל מן רקיעא
והוא הכנא
וקרא אלהא לרקיעא: שמיא
והוא רמשא
והוא צפרא
יומא דתרין

ואמר אלהא:
נתכנשון מיא דלתחת מן שמיא
לאתרא חד
ותתחזא יבישתא
והוא הכנא
וקרא אלהא ליבישתא: ארעא
ולכנשא דמיא קרא: יממא
וחזא אלהא דשפיר

ואמר אלהא:
תפק ארעא תדאא
עסבא דמזדרע זרעא לגנסה
ואילנא דפארא דעבד פארא
דנצבתה בה
על ארעא
והוא הכנא
ואפקת ארעא תדאא
עסבא דמזדרע זרעא לגנסה

33

ואילנא דעבד פארא
דלצבתה בה לגנסה
וחזא אלהא דשפיר
והוא רמשא
והוא צפרא
יומא דתלתא

ואמר אלהא:
נהוון נהירא ברקילא דשמיא
למפרש בית איממא לליליא:
ונהוון לאתותא
ולזבנא וליומתא
ולשניא
ונהוון מנהרין
ברקיעא דשמיא
למנהרו על ארעא
והוא הכנא
ועבד אלהא תרין נהירא רורבא
נהירא רבא לשולטנא דאיממא
ונהירא זעורא לשנלטנא דלליא
וכוכבא
ויהב אנן אלהא ברקיעא דשמיא
למנהרו על ארעא
ולמשלט באיממא
ובלליא
ולמפרש בית נהירא לנישוכא
וחזא אלהא דשפיר
והוא רמשא
והוא צפרא
יומא דארבעא

34

וַאֲמַר אֱלָהָא:
נִרְחֲשׁוּן מַיָּא
רַחֲשָׁא נַפְשָׁא חַיְתָא
וּפָרַחְתָּא תְּפָרַח עַל אַרְעָא
אֲלָאפֵי רְקִיעָא דִשְׁמַיָּא
אֲבָרָא אֱלָהָא תַּנִּינַא רוֹרְבָא
וְכָל נַפְשָׁא חַיְתָא דְּרַחֲשָׁא
דְּאַרְחִשׁוּ מַיָּא לִגְנַסְהוֹן
וְחָלְפָרַחְתָּא דְּגַפָא לִגְנַסָא
וַחֲזָא אֱלָהָא דִּשְׁפִיר
וּבָרֵךְ אָנוּן אֱלָהָא
וַאֲמַר לְהוֹן
פְּרוּ וּסְגוּ
וּמְלוֹ מַיָּא דְּבְיַמְמָא
וּפָרַחְתָּא תִּסְבָּא בְּאַרְעָא
וַהֲוָא רַמְשָׁא
וַהֲוָא צַפְרָא
יוֹמָא דַחֲמִשָּׁא

וַאֲמַר אֱלָהָא:
תַּפֵּק אַרְעָא נַפְשָׁא חַיְתָא
לִגְנַסַהּ
בְּעִירָא וְרַחֲשָׁא וְ;יוּתָא דְּאַרְעָא
לִגְנַסַהּ
וַהֲוָא הֲכַנָא
וַעֲבַד אֱלָהָא חֵיוָתָא דְּאַרְעָא
לִגְנַסַהּ
וּבְעִירָא לִגְנַסַהּ
וְכָלֵהּ רַחֲשָׁא דְּאַרְעָא
לִגְנַסַהּ
אַחֲזָא אֱלָהָא דִּשְׁפִיר

ואמר אלהא:
נעבד אנשא בצלמן
איך דמותן
ונשלטון בנוני ימא
ובפרחתא דשמיא
ובבעירא
ובכלה חיותא דארעא
ובכלה דרחשא
דרחש על ארעא
וברא אלהא לאדם
בצלמה
בצלם אלהא
ברימי
דכר ונאבא
ברא אנון
וברך אנון אלהא
ואמר להון אלהא:
פרו וסגו
ומלו ארעא וכובשוה
ושלטו בנוני ימא
ובפחתא דשמיא
ובבעירא
ובכלה חיותא דרחשא על ארעא

ואמר אלהא:
הא יהבת לכון כלה עסבא דזרעא
דמזדרע על אפי כלה ארעא
וכל אילן דאית בה פארי אילנה
דזרעה מזדרא
לכון נהוא למאכולתא
ולכלה חיותא דדברא

ולכלה פרחתא דשמיא
ולכל דרחש על ארעא
דאית בה נפשא חיתא
וכלה יורקא דעסבא למאכולתא
והוא הכנא

וחזא אלהא כל
דכבד
והא
טב שפיר
והוא רמשא
והוא זפרא
יומא דשתתא

ושלמו שמיא וארעא
וכלה חילהון
ושלם אלהא
ביומא שתיתיא עבדוהי
דעבד
ואתתניני בימוא שביעיא
מן כלהון עבדוהי דעבד
וברך אלהא ליומא שביעיא
וקדשה
מטל דבה
אתתניני מן כלהון עבדוהי
דברא אלהא למעבד

Chapter 3

THE PRIMEVAL MYSTERY

The Genesis record of creation (Gen. 1–2:3) is a profound and compelling description of a primeval event. It is a sacred Hebrew narration that gives meaning to the heavens, the earth, and humankind in their present existence. Since it is a cosmogonic composition, the composer places emphasis on God, the Creator.

Elohim speaks the creative magisterial word, and form appears. God not only creates but brings about order wherever there is disorder, which is structuring order in the midst of chaos.[1] *Elohim*-God (Aramaic: *alaha*), the creator, is not only the maker of heaven and earth, but is also the Lord God (Hebrew: *yahweh*[2] *elohim*). The One who is ever present with all His creation as the immanent is also the One who is the universal Deity.

Genesis 1:1–2:3 is not a modern treatise on creation. Nonetheless, in the light of present-day cosmological theories one could interpret the narrative from a scientific viewpoint.[3]

---

[1]Not surprisingly, the same creative energy that brings about order out of chaos is also indicative of the creative soul-force within each of us. This divine energy persistently brings about order and wholeness within ourselves, i.e., a harmonious polycentricity of life.

[2]The Hebrew name of God is usually rendered in English as *yhwh* (consonants only). No one knows how to pronounce the ancient name. The pronunciation *yahweh* is a scholarly guess. See subheadings of this chapter, "*yahweh*" and "*ehyeh*" for detailed descriptions of the divine name.

[3]For an interesting and literal scientific explanation of Gen. 1–2:3, see Nathan Aviezer, *In the Beginning: Biblical Creation and Science*.

It is a sacred presentation of the cosmos that is both mystical and metaphysical. (I use the term "mystical" in the sense of "mystery.") I believe that what makes the biblical narrative remain such an impelling mystery for most of us is its disarming directness and depth.

Let us recall that the Hebrew narrator offers a moving and imaginative portrayal of the heavens, the earth and its environment, the animal world and humanity. He poetically writes his message, affirming God's active energies, which underlie all phenomena.

When the writer penned the creation narrative, the major part of the populace could not read or write. They relied on their scribes and learned men to read and interpret holy Scripture for them. Hebrew and Aramaic manuscripts of the Bible were written in a deliberate poetic style so that, when the texts were read aloud, they would express a specific emphasis. Rhythm, sound, continuous and expanding repetition, allusions, and wordplay were extremely important. Listeners to a reading of the holy text were meant to hear and feel the narratives taking hold of them. The poetic word-play and well-chosen picture-words captured their hearts and minds. For example, Gen. 1:1-2:3 expresses the creative orderliness of six days in a direct, simple, repetitive, sensual manner and language.[4] This mode of writing creates for the listener and the reader a visual, suspenseful drama engaging all the senses and making the read-

---

[4]Not only is Gen. 1:1–2:3 stylized in this manner, but the entire Bible in its original tongue of Hebrew and its sister Semitic language Aramaic follows the same pattern. Most of the book of Genesis is sacred legend and folklore literature.

er/listener hang on every word. It is the power and charm of ancient storytelling at its best.

The engrossing creation epic, masterfully woven by the biblical poet, challenges our imaginations to an awe-inspiring encounter. We come face to face with our elusive, mysterious universe which leaves us in wonder. Then we also encounter an equally mysterious Intelligence we call "God." The poet explains nothing; he simply delivers his impressive, descriptive creation narrative.

A WORLD OF MYSTERY

We of today are beset by much cynicism, which can hurt and cripple us. The present lifestyle of our society places enormous emphasis on acquiring material goods. We are further ensnared by narrow mental awareness of "specialized" areas of knowledge. This specialization subtly creates an insensitivity to the mysterious beauty that surrounds us and exists within us. Because of these conditions, we can easily lose responsiveness to the wonder of being alive in a world full of mystery. Despite all the empirical knowledge and startling advances we have gained from our varied theologies and sciences, God and creation remain a mystery. Our explorations and studies seem to deepen the mysteries of creation, yielding even more provocative inquiries which are endless.

Our evolving and changing theologies goad us into deeper wonderment; so much so that we wonder why and how anything exists at all! We cannot expect any single field of study to provide all the answers for us be it science, religion, philosophy, psychology, or metaphysics. The best our rational minds can do is create new modalities for the appearance of the universe and the phenomenon of humankind. Our present explanations of the primeval creation event provoke further inquiry and still leave us with our imaginations stunned. The universe does not work the way we had figured it out.[5] To quote J. B. S. Haldane, "The universe is not only queerer than we imagine, but it is queerer than we can imagine."[6]

WHERE ARE WE?

Have you ever asked yourself, "Where are we?" Where we are is very much a mystery. We know that we live on a planet that we call Earth. It is in a galaxy of planets that scientists have named the Milky Way, which exists somewhere in a universe of galaxies. Modern Science reports that the universe is expanding and that space is curved. The challenge here is that there is no beginning or ending point in this universe of galaxies from which we can measure the vast expanse of populated space.

Psychologically we feel we know where we are because we have named the area, or the place, in which we reside. We also feel comfortable by setting parameters. However, naming a place and setting boundaries does not really tell us where we are. For instance, when one crosses the border from Arizona to California, the land does not know it has been divided and its name changed. Naming places and things is a convenience we have invented out of necessity to simplify communication.

---

[5]See Werner Heisenberg, *Physics & Philosophy: The Revolution in Modern Science*.

[6]See Fred Alan Wolf, *Taking the Quantum Leap*, p. 100, "No One Has Seen the Wind."

The reality is this: places and things are nameless. To quote Max Muller, philosopher, "Things are thinks."

There are those, of course, who attempt to answer philosophically and religiously the question, "Where are we?" Often, when I lecture on the subject of creation, I ask my listeners to answer this question for me. The audience is generally quick to reply with learned, metaphysical, or philosophical conditioned responses such as: "We are here," "We are in God," "We are in the now!"

These responses usually engender more probing questions: "Where is here?" "Where in God?" ("What is God?") "Where and what is the now?" All answers, no matter how plausible they may be to the rational mind, tend to dissipate as mere diversions when examined closely. They do not provide us with deeply satisfying solutions because this type of inquiry demands our entire being to participate in its resolve.

We cannot honestly and truly give an answer to "Where are we?" As unbelievable as this is going to seem to us, we have to face the fact that we are lost! It is, no doubt, utterly humbling for us to realize that we don't know where we are. Not only is this incredible to ponder, but it is just as staggering to imagine how our being is possible at all! In other words, our human presence is an enigma! If we deeply perceive this realization it becomes the beginning of wisdom and the ending of arrogance. We are restored to a childlike state of wonder, inquisitiveness, sensitivity and responsiveness to ourselves and everything around us.

We truly exist in a vast, expansive, mysterious universe of which we know so little in spite of our ever increasing knowledge in the fields of science, metaphysics, theology, archeology, and anthropology. Our state of being is a great mystery. Even our so-called "physical" forms are a great wonder and mystery to us. And what is so astounding is that our lives are also a mystery!

MATTER AND SUBSTANCE

Terms such as "physical," "material," "matter," are convenient language labels that we place on the appearance of the world and all things in it, including our bodily forms. According to Alan Keightley, a Christian philosopher, reality and descriptions of such, like "physical" and "material" are in themselves philosophical ideas. He says that our thoughts fragment the world and goes on to tell us:

> *Physical* and *material* are words we use to talk **about** the world. The world as it is in itself is unspeakable. The words we use about the world embody our conventional ways of thinking. Conventions are 'conveniences' and we readily acknowledge this to be the case in systems of measurement, legal and social customs, and so on. . . . There are no things in the world. Things are terms, not entities. All things, facts and events are simplified, convenient units of perception and attention."[7]

In the science of quantum physics, physical form, or matter is not considered a solid substance. Nothing that has been termed or called basic in the universe is, in reality, fixed and motionless.[8]

---

[7]Alan Keightley, *Into Every Life a Little Zen Must Fall*, p. 74.

[8]See Fred Alan Wolf, *Taking the Quantum Leap*, "Wave-Particle Duality and the Principle of Complementarity," pp. 133–41.

We inhabit a viable planet that also is a mystery. In a wonderful and meaningful manner our luxuriant and versatile Mother Earth gives birth to us. She literally grows us as we feed off her verdant plants, flourishing crops, and oxygenated atmosphere. All this unanswered is-ness inspires deep reverence and respect for life in all its myriad animate and inanimate forms. The biblical writer does not help us solve any mysteries of creation. He instead introduces us to the creator of these mysteries.

ANCIENT BELIEF

In Genesis 1:1 the Near Eastern author puts emphasis on God: "In the beginning **God** created the heavens and the earth." It is no accident that the author begins his narrative with this kind of emphasis. To a Semite, God is first and above all. Religion and belief in God are an all-consuming reality. Dr. Abraham Rihbany, a prolific writer on the Near East, states this point very clearly:

> The supreme choice of the Oriental [Semite] has been religion. To say that this choice has not been altogether a conscious one, that it has been the outcome of temperament, does by no means lessen its significance. From the beginning of his history on the earth to this day the Oriental [Semite] has been conscious above all things of two supreme realities — *God* and the *soul*.[9]

This deeply ingrained attitude of complete reliance upon God goes far back in the history of the people of the Near East.

---

[9]Abraham M. Rihbany, *The Syrian Christ*, p. 84.

In those ancient days, nomadic and seminomadic tribes were totally dependent upon their gods for survival. Wandering tribes needed a god to guide them to hidden wells, grazing areas, and other food sources. Merchants sold idols in the market-places, and every clan had a god. Families had great ancestral gods made of stone and wood. They carried their gods and goddesses on the backs of camels, horses, and donkeys. Occasionally priests bore them on their shoulders. Sometimes these handmade idols (gods) were stolen by rival tribes and broken into pieces. These clans would fight to the last man in defense of their handcrafted images.

Ancient tribal peoples needed their idols because their faith in these gods helped them to travel the vast trackless deserts and uncharted lands of the Near East. They had a deep inner knowledge that was guiding them through the lands. Yet, simultaneously, they felt mysterious nature forces emanating from the heavens and all around them. These tribes, by relying upon their idol-gods and star-gods, could receive oracles and guidance that met their needs. This was their method of tapping into and making use of their natural innate human abilities.

THE MYSTERY OF GOD'S ORIGIN

From where does the God of Israel or, shall we ask, the God of the Bible originate? The origin of the biblical or national God of Israel could be discussed intellectually and argued from the perspective of Canaanite and Mesopotamian myths.[10] To put it simply, much of the Near Eastern mythic lore and ideas has been transformed by the Hebrew authors of the Bible.

Besides the biblical and Near Eastern theogonic accounts of God's being, where else may we turn for an understanding of the "origin of God?" This question could easily be construed as presumptuous, if not ridiculous as well. But even children ask this very same question in simpler words: "Who made God?" Whether the reader considers this question to be presumptuous or ridiculous, it still troubles those who search for understanding. There are also those who have dismissed the idea of God from their minds completely. Therefore they do not dwell on the question of God's origin. For the sake of understanding, let us refer to God as the "Profound" and the "Sacred."[11]

What we really need to ask ourselves is: "Can human beings come to know the origin of the deeply Sacred and the infinitely Profound?" It is a misconception to think that through thought alone we can capture and enshrine the Profound. To truly understand and realize the Sacred, one must be willing to free all thought about God. Thought does not originate the Sacred and Profound. Nonetheless, it does attempt to define what is Sacred and Profound. Thought also

---

[10]See Conrad E. L'Heureux, "Searching for the origins of God" pp. 33–57 of *Traditions in Transformation: Turning Points in Biblical Faith*, Halpern and Levenson, eds. For further research, see Mark S. Smith, *The Early History of God and Other Deities in Ancient Israel* and Tryggve N. D. Mettinger, *In Search of God: The Meaning and Message of the Everlasting Names* tr. Frederick H. Cryer. For additional material, I refer you to the Bibliography.

[11]See subheadings: "The Term God," "What's in a Name," *"ehyeh,"* *"yahweh,"* and *"el shaddai"* for discussion of the names of God used to denote different aspects of the nature of God.

47

creates stories to give dimension to God and may also cast the Divine within a human context. However, the Profound and the Sacred are truly without dimension and go beyond the context of thought. If we are to realize the infinitely Profound, conceptual thinking must be temporarily suspended. "God" is beyond functional thought, but not beyond human consciousness or the sensitivity of the human soul.

Many deep experiences in life are extremely difficult to define or capture with words alone. For instance, how can one explain with mere words the depth of love and care a mother and father have for their children? Or how can one explain the mysterious bond of love? Love defies definition. In reality, almost anything of a profoundly deep nature defies definition. Metaphorical poetry helps, but, alas, it is only a description. There exist certain realizations which occur in human consciousness that cannot be fully comprehended, but that can be apprehended.

GOD AND THE HUMAN SOUL

The Bible tells us nothing about the origin of God.[12] Nevertheless, for me, God does not literally originate in the heavens above us, but in the imaginal "heavens" of the human soul. I use the adjective *imaginal* in the same sense as the French Islamic scholar Henry Corbin has coined it. He used the word *imaginal* to distinguish it from the negative and

---

[12]This is not only true for the origin of God, but also for biblical personages who just suddenly appear and nothing is told of their origin or life. For example, see the prophet Elijah, 1 Ki. 17:1–24. Most of the so-called "origin" biographies (which are few) are folklore and legends.

belittling connotation "imaginary." The holy temple of the human heart embraces what is Sacred and Profound in life. Yet, the soul cannot capture it in the sense of holding it a prisoner.

Compare the human soul to the seed of a living plant — for example, an apple seed. Hidden in this seed is the pattern of the apple tree. No one can see the apple tree just by looking at the seed, but it is there nevertheless. Similarly, hidden in the human soul is the presence of Spirit — God. I do not mean by this illustration that the soul encompasses the Spirit. For the Spirit encompasses not only the soul but the entire universe. One can readily see how difficult it is to explain what is truly wordless and indescribable. Philosophically, what is unknowable has to be spoken or explained in terms of what is known, and is therefore linguistically limited.

Even when we speak about researching the early history or origin of God, we really are speaking about researching an idea of God. God itself is never an idea; explanations of God are ideas.

The term "God" is a language symbol that points to a reality that is beyond words. For instance, the term "tree" is only a word and not the "tree" itself. The word simply points to the idea of a "tree." So, then, the term "God" is not God itself; it only suggests an idea of God. Reality transcends language and can be realized only in human consciousness.

WHAT IS GOD?

Today God is known as the unseen creator and originator of all things, the Supreme Provider, the Supreme Being. Nevertheless, we still ask, "What is God?" We humans have the capacity to feel an invisible presence that we call divine, but words again fail us in our attempt to explain the inexplicable. Yet we continue to speak of "God" as Eternal Spirit, the Omniscient, the Omnipotent, the Omnipresent, and the Omniactive.

The writers of Scripture teach that God's nature is unconditional love and peace. They also inform us that God may act as a man who becomes angry, happy, and who also repents and becomes sorry for His mistakes. And at the same time, we are taught that God is unchangeable and that no condition can possibly affect the divine nature.

Why, then, do the writers of Scripture depict God with human emotional characteristics and with the capacity to succeed or fail? Primarily, we need to understand that the Creator cannot be described or defined by His creations. Secondarily, the word "God" is a metaphysical term. Therefore the biblical poets, prophets, and scribes pictured and presented the God of Israel as a man. They described him as a passionate Semite who expressed himself within the context of their Near Eastern culture. God is presented by these biblical authors as a great Eastern potentate surrounded by messengers (angels), viziers and other heavenly officials. Thus these writers humanized and characterized God as an Easterner and, in particular, as a Semite.

Metaphysical concepts are difficult for us to understand. I like to compare metaphysical and spiritual ideas to liquids and gases. One needs containers to carry liquids and gases from one place to another. Thus, in the Bible, the parables, allegories, legends, and symbolic and metaphorical language are the "containers" that carry metaphysical concepts and spiritual ideas of the ineffable (God). Thus, for us or any modern thinker, the "containers" of the Bible are better understood in a nonliteral sense. This is especially true when reading those verses that are descriptive of a human God with human attributes.

Since "God" has been described as a great Near Eastern sovereign by Hebrew authors, then it makes sense that *yahweh elohim* must be feared as such. The Semitic word translated as "fear" is often misunderstood. The Aramaic word *dighlta* carries more meaning than just "being afraid." In many passages of Scripture this word *dighlta* should be translated as "revere" or "respect." Reverence and respect do not refer to being fearful or frightened. Both these characteristics come from our aesthetic qualities and affinity with our spiritual nature. "Reverence is one of man's answers to the presence of mystery." [13]

In the Near East, God is revered because He is known as "creator" and "father." But, we may ask, "Whatever happened to the role of mother?" "What about creative feminine acts?" In the myths of ancient Iraq (Sumer and Akkad), gods and goddesses were very important.[14] They reflected the major roles men and women played in that society. There also existed many traditional versions of the creation of humanity by mother-goddesses and personal feminine deities that cared for and looked after the populace. What the Hebrew poetic authors and narrators did was alter and transform these feminine myths for their own use in the Bible.[15] They attributed and assigned many feminine roles and activities that had

---

[13]Abraham Joshua Heschel.

[14]That is, before the goddesses were marginalized and eclipsed by the roles of the gods.

[15]See Tikva Frymer-Kensky, *In the Wake of the Goddesses: Women, Culture and the Biblical Transformation of Pagan Myth.*

been performed by the goddesses to *yahweh*.[16]   Thus, the
LORD God (*yahweh elohim*) may be thought of as divine
parent, father-mother God, when performing certain duties.
Jesus describes God as a parent, a father who cares for and
guides his beloved children. He also describes God as a caring
shepherd continually seeking those who, like sheep, may stray
and healing those who may be injured, bruised, or ill.

When the question "What is God?" comes to mind, we
may also ask, "What is God *not*?" Is there anyplace in the
universe where God is not present or anything which is not
sustained by the power and wisdom of the Supreme Being?
According to Scripture, this power is in all and through all.
This efficacious Presence may be sensed in a blade of grass, a
tree, a mountain, in the stars and in a human being. God is all
and through all, but is also beyond all. We may say, then, that
God is both immanent and transcendent. But have we ade-
quately answered the question "What is God?"

A PARABLE

There is a story told about a philosopher-monk who
attempted to find an answer to "What is God?" He decided to
withdraw from society and put himself in isolation and solitude.

---

[16]*Yahweh* assumed the roles that had been assigned to mother goddesses
who usually took care of women during the process of gestation and
childbirth. In monotheism there is no longer a need for divine midwife-
helpers or divine labor-assistants. The Lord God of Israel took over the
entire process from conception to birth. See Ps. 139:13–16; Isa. 44:2, 24;
Job 31:15; Isa. 46:3–4; Isa. 66:9; Also see Phyllis Trible, *God and the
Rhetoric of Sexuality: From the Wombs of Women to the Compassion of God*.
pp. 34–56.

For many months he lived in a cave near a beautiful lake, searching earnestly for the answer to this haunting question. After having spent some time alone and completely absorbed and concentrated on his quest, the seeker discovered that there was a monastery just across the lake. The abbot of the monastery had heard about the quest that this philosopher-monk had undertaken. He knew that the philosopher was living nearby and was trying to solve the engrossing, enigmatic question "What is God?"

One day the abbot sent a message inviting the philosopher to the monastery to break bread with him. The recluse seeker was glad to receive the warm invitation and accepted the request to visit the abbey.

Now, on the day that the philosopher was to arrive, the head of the monastery changed his apparel and dressed himself in simple peasant garments. He also wore a cowl that partly hid his face. The abbot quickly exited the monastery and went to the area of the lake that was near the cave where the seeking monk resided. When the disguised abbot saw the contemplative thinker leaving his cave and walking alongside the lake on his way to the monastery, he took a wooden spoon from his pocket, dipped it in the lake, and filled it with water. Then he took a few steps backward and poured the water from the spoon on the ground. The abbot continued repeating this unusual and amusing behavior.

The philosopher, strolling along the shore, saw this strange scene and thought the poor peasant to be out of his mind. He approached the poorly clad man cautiously and asked, "What are you trying to do?" The stranger replied, "Sir, I am trying to empty the lake so that when one travels, one can take a shortcut." The philosopher in a loud and surprised tone replied, "You're crazy! How can you empty this great lake with that small wooden spoon?" The disguised abbot quickly answered, "I understand you're living in that cave trying to comprehend the incomprehensible, to fathom the unfathomable, and to measure the measureless. You do this with your little head, which is even smaller than my wooden spoon, when you compare the task you have undertaken with that of my present task." Then the philosopher suddenly realized that the sea he was trying to cross was shoreless and endless. He decided to abandon the entire quest and so went happily with the abbot to have a good meal.

A human being is endowed with the wisdom to be aware of his or her function and expression in life. Basic to life is self-discovery. When we perceive and become our true and essential self, we also realize our creator. Intuitively we know that the quest for ourselves is the quest for God (Spirit), and the quest for God is the quest for ourselves.

Jesus told the Samaritan woman that "God is spirit." The term "spirit," *ruha*, in Aramaic has many meanings such as "wind," "vibration," "temper," "universal," "everywhere," and "all-embracing." Spirit cannot be photographed, grasped, measured, or numbered. It has no dimension and is infinitesimal and indivisible. Spirit is formless and yet can manifest itself in any form or manner. Human language cannot explain "spirit," but inwardly one can feel and hear spirit's inarticulate voice. It was through the "spirit" that the Hebrew writers and prophets communed with "God" and heard the inner voice.

GOD — THE MYSTERY

I would like to relate an interesting encounter that I had aboard a jetliner. It happened many years ago when I was

54

returning from an intense and fatiguing speaking tour. I was attempting to relax and enjoy the flight when I felt a sudden tap on my shoulder. A stranger, who occupied the aisle seat, had noticed my books, which were lying on the seat between us. He questioned me about their religious content. From that point on we began to chat.

He told me he was a physicist and an astronomer. Our conversation deepened. He paused for a moment and then emphatically and emotionally declared, "I don't believe in God!" I did not reply to his energetic, emotionally charged words, but continued discussing the different religious philosophies contained in the books. Again, he reiterated his feelings and exclaimed: "I don't believe in God!" Evidently, he was looking for some sort of retort or shock response. I paused for a few moments, then looked upward as if seeing God. I opened my palms and extended my hands upward and out toward my new-found friend — and with a shrug of my shoulders, I casually and lightheartedly responded, "If it hasn't bothered God all this time, why should it bother me?"

The expression on his face was both amazement and amusement. He was surprised that I would make such a comment! He said to me, "You're different." I then began to ask him how he felt when he surveyed the heavens. At first he gave me scientific explanations and jargon. I asked him again, "How do you *feel* when you probe the universe?" He sat back, relaxed, and said with a smile, "It blows my mind." I quickly responded, "Now we're talking about God."

God couldn't care less whether we believe in a self-existent presence. Biblically speaking, belief in God had nothing to do with the question of the existence of God.[17] In

---

[17]See Chapter 1, subheading "The Ancient Near East."

55

the Near East, people simply believed in the existence of a god or gods. In the scriptural sense, belief in God determined one's ethical behavior. That is, to "believe in God " meant that one followed the Torah.

Earlier I said that despite the tremendous explosion of empirical data which has revealed many secrets of the universe, the universe is still as much a mystery as God is a mystery. Our present ideas about God, the universe and humankind are fascinating conceptual classifications. These classifications are interpretations. God and the universe, in themselves, are inexplicable. The words of Abraham J. Heschel express this idea so clearly: "Concepts are delicious snacks with which we try to alleviate our amazement."[18]

Let us recall that when we describe our universe, the earth and the "things" in it, we must use certain language symbols — "physical," "matter," "form," and so forth. Such words are helpful terminologies that conceptualize our world. However, let us also remember that the reality of the world far surpasses our ideas, thoughts, and descriptions of it. We live in an endless, limitless and shoreless universe. Spiritually, there is no distance to conquer and no chasm to bridge.

CONCEPTS ABOUT GOD

When we study our immense universe, our minds are overwhelmed by its vastness. In our attempt to encompass and comprehend God only on a mental level, we produce the same

---

[18]Abraham J. Heschel, *Man is not Alone: A Philosophy of Religion*, "The Disparity of Soul and Reason," p. 7.

mind-boggling experience as when we try to mentally encompass the universe.[19]

We run head-on into difficulties when we attempt to reduce God to ideas only. Although concepts are meaningful and helpful, they are definitely limited. They are interpretative reaches for something that cannot be grasped by the intellect exclusively. However, we can realize the presence and reality of a Supreme Being without trying to grasp that reality. God and the universe truly dwell in a wordless dimension.

It needs to be stated again that interpretations of God fall short of what God is. This is because a deity would have to be described in terms of what is known. When we try to explain God through the known manifestations of creation, it is like trying to explain the existence of the sun through one of its rays. "God" is indescribable in physical terms or ideas because God is greater than any of the concepts one may hold. Logical thinking creates concepts that only render a partial picture. God will always remain a mystery for rational thinking alone. When we attempt to explain God rationally, it is like trying to store ice in a hot oven or fire in a freezer.

Despite this difficulty, God can be perceived through intellectual, nonsensory intuition. In philosophy this is known as a Noumenon. In other words, though God cannot be seen, God can be understood on an intuitive level — beyond limited rational patterns.

God speaks without words. However, God is not the only silent speaker in our universe. The earth and all nature communicate without words. Again, it needs to be stated that Spirit is beyond the realms of mathematical equation and Newtonian physics. Spiritual realization and revelation are

---

[19]Op. cit., "The Mystery within Reason," pp. 13, 14.

primary channels open to us through which we perceive, at least partially, the nature and existence of God. Through revelation one can know the power, presence and greatness of God.

We have the capacity to know and commune with God's presence and understand His attributes because they are inherent within us. This is how we come to know the nature of God, His goodness and love. Matthew, in his gospel, reports Jesus as having taught that any person with a "pure heart" (clear mind) has the capacity and power to "see [perceive] God." "Delighted are those who are pure in their hearts [sincere] for they shall see [perceive] God."[20]

THE TERM "GOD"

We can gain some insight about what the term "God" meant to the biblical writers by defining its Semitic root meaning. The Aramaic word *alaha*, the Hebrew word *elohim*, and the Arabic word *allah* for "God" are assumed to be derived from the Semitic root *elh*. There are several mainline theories about the meaning of this root in Semitic languages. (1) The strong or mighty one, (2) the revered one, (3) the highest one (Canaanite root), (4) helper, supporter, one who sustains (Aramaic root).

Another Aramaic term for God is *ithea*, "self-existent," "self-cohesive and sustaining." This term is qualitative and refers to the eternal existence, i.e., something that exists of itself and does not derive its life anywhere, or through anything else.

---

[20] Mt. 5:8, Aramaic Peshitta Text, Errico translation. See Rocco A. Errico, *The Message of Matthew: An Annotated Parallel Aramaic-English Gospel of Matthew*.

In other words, God is all there is. Everything we call "a thing" derives its existence from *ithea*.[21]

The self-existent principle known as *ithea* in Aramaic is the efficacious creative presence. This presence permeates and acts within the continual expansion of the universe and, as such, appears to us as "impersonal." Apparently this "impersonal" principle is active within every member of the human family.[22] It effectively keeps us on the move, evolving our maturity and individuality. Thus one might say *ithea* becomes personal within each individual and is not just a "principle" within us. (The term "individual" does not mean separateness, but comes from the Latin root meaning to be indivisible and undivided. Therefore, individuality is a constant state of maturing.)

OTHER ASPECTS OF GOD

In the Book of Exodus, Chapter Three, we are introduced to a new expression of the presence of God. It was a new insight for Moses, the great Hebrew prophet and lawgiver. Moses had been tending the flock of Jethro, his father-in-law, the Midianite priest. He had been leading the sheep from Jethro's home, and he passed through a desert area before reaching the pasture land of Horeb. Biblical scholars usually describe this pastoral area as "the most elevated ground of the peninsula." You find the most fertile valleys in which even fruit trees grow. Water abounds in this district; consequently it is the resort of all Bedouins when the lower countries are dried up.

---

[21]Note: *ITHEA* implies "it," "origin." See Chapter 4, under the subheading "Causality."

[22]This does not preclude its activity in animal or plant life.

It was here in Horeb at a certain mountain that God summoned and commissioned Moses to deliver his people from Egypt. The messenger of *yahweh* appeared in a burning bush, and Moses conversed with God. "Now Moses said to God: 'Behold, I am going to the Israelites and I will tell them, The Lord God of your fathers has sent me to you; then they will ask me, What is his name? Now what shall I say to them?' Then God said to Moses: '*aheeyah-ashar-aheeyah*' (Hebrew '*ehyeh-asher-ehyeh*'). And this is what you shall say to the Israelites, '*aheeyah*' ('*ehyeh*') has sent me to you."[23]

WHAT'S IN A NAME?

In the world of the ancient Near East, names of gods and goddesses, and names in general, were believed to possess a vital quality. Names were very important not just for identification, but because they were expressive of power and character. According to some of these primitive myths, the gods jealously guarded their precious names. Knowing a god's name gave one power and access to that deity. Names represented the nature, position, and function of the gods and goddesses.

Moses suggested to God that the Israelites would want to know the name of the deity that had commissioned him to deliver them from the hands of the Egyptians. But it is more likely that Moses wanted to learn the name of the deity so that he could approach God himself. Let us recall that knowledge

---

[23]Ex. 3:14–15, Aramaic Peshitta Text, Errico translation. (Note: I purposely did not translate the divine name but transliterated it from Aramaic (*aheeyah*) and from Hebrew (*ehyeh*). It is usually translated as "I AM.")

60

of a deity's or individual's name provided for the seeker access to, and a measure of power over, that god, goddess, or individual. It was believed that the name contained the power and character of the possessor. For Moses, knowing the divine name was his path to the Presence.[24]

EHYEH

The divine name *ehyeh* is believed by most scholars to be the first person singular of the Hebrew verb "to be" (*hayah*). This verb implies both the present and the future. The translation of the divine name *ehyeh* as "I am" is disputed by Hebrew grammarians. This phrase *ehyeh-asher-ehyeh* becomes even more complicated because of the doubling of the name *ehyeh*. As an example, the first *ehyeh* might be one form of the tense, such as "I am" and the second might be "I will be." The Hebrew word *asher* can mean "who," "what," or "that which."

However, modern commentators conclude that the translation of the name as "I am" does not carry the full meaning of *ehyeh*. They propose that *ehyeh* in both instances implies the future tense of the verb *hayah* and translate its meaning as: "I will be what tomorrow demands."[25] (J. D. Levenson suggests "I shall be where I shall be.")[26] In other

---

[24]Moses never employed this form of the divine name *ehyeh* among the Hebrews, but the derivative: *yahweh*. Thus, the revelation of the name was really for Moses' sake. It was extremely important for him and for a new stage of development in the history of monotheism.

[25]W. Gunther Plaut, *The Torah: A Modern Commentary*, vol. II, "The Divine Name *ehyeh*" pp. 39–41.

[26]Jon D. Levenson, *Sinai & Zion: An Entry into the Jewish Bible*.

words, *ehyeh* or *yahweh*, the God of Israel, is totally free and unconfined by any parameters that the human mind may establish. After all, *yahweh* was a boundless god of the desert. Then again, there are others who also interpret the biblical phrase as: "I will be who I will be," and this is explained as "He who is essentially unnameable, inexplicable, and indescribable." In the Jewish writings of the Midrash the following is suggested: "While God is called by many names, He is what He is by virtue of His deeds. That is to say, you cannot really know Him until you experience Him in your lives."

Although scriptures tell us that God had made Himself known to Moses as to no other human being, the full depth and significance of the name *ehyeh*, for the present, must remain elusive. Besides its technical meaning, for me there is a practical application here. If this interpretation of the scriptural passage "I will be what tomorrow demands" is a reliable one, then the divine name is of great significance for us also and not just for Moses or for the developing monotheism of ancient Israel.

The divine appellation *ehyeh-asher-ehyeh*, may be understood to mean that God is and will always be the fulfillment of every human being. In other words, what we come to realize from this recording of the divine name is that spiritual forces that reside within every individual can and do respond to human need. God as infinite, loving, intelligent presence in the human family is, and will always be, whatever is needed of It.

YAHWEH

There is also a second time in the book of Exodus (Ex. 6:2-3) that the divine name is revealed to Moses. But here, instead of the name *ehyeh*, it is another form of the verb *hayah* and that is *yahweh*. Biblical scholars propose that both Chapter Six and Chapter Three, which present facets of God's name and nature, are most likely variant traditions of the same motif. Let us now consider the divine designation *yhwh*.[27]

"And the Lord spoke with Moses and said to him: I am the Lord (Hebrew *yhwh*). I appeared to Abraham, Isaac, and Jacob as God, the almighty God [*el*[28] *shaddai*]; but the name of Lord [Hebrew *yhwh*] I did not make known to them."[29] According to most Semitic experts the divine name *yahweh* is believed to be the third person singular of the Hebrew verb "to be" (*hayah*),[30] a causative form of the verb which would translate as "He who causes to be."[31] We have learned that we may come to understand various aspects of God's being and presence through the divine names. The sacred names of God in Hebrew Scripture gave birth to and deepened the perception of the fundamentals of monotheism.

------

[27]See footnote 1 of this chapter.

[28]The God "*el*" of the Hebrew patriarchs Abraham, Isaac, and Jacob was not like other deities of that time. The gods of that age were stationary and motionless idols, i.e., they were confined to certain localities and ruled over particular territories. The God of the patriarchs was mobile and not limited to any local shrine or high place.

[29]Ex. 6:2–3. Aramaic Peshitta Text, Errico translation.

[30]See subheading in this chapter "What's in a Name," paragraph 2, the divine name *ehyeh*.

[31]However, there are several other scholarly opinions based on exhaustive analysis of verb forms in Babylonian and Canaanite languages — "He who indeed will [show himself to] be," or "He who proves himself." There are at least five or six more possible renderings of *ehyeh*, but of all of them, I find the one translated from Hebrew by Martin Buber and Franz Rosenzweig most appealing: "He is present [with you]." In Aramaic the name signifies "He who brings into being," "life-giver," and "giver of existence."

63

But there is something more important for us to consider than just the relationship between the divine names and monotheism. Human beings like you and me experienced the reality of these names. Their souls responded to and interacted with the divine Presence they felt was guiding them. This experience went beyond any intellectual comprehension. The recipients were nourished in the deep recesses of their beings.

According to the Exodus story, God previously told Moses that He was to be understood as *ehyeh-asher-ehyeh*. We have discovered that there are many possibilities with the term *ehyeh*, such as, the "self-existent God," "the boundless one," "the one who is, was and will be," i.e., "He who has within Himself inexhaustible resources of being," i.e., being whatever He wishes to be.

From another perspective, one can say that God cannot be fully defined by an event, circumstance, or by the experiences of any one individual, clan, generation, nation, or age. The divine presence endlessly renews the revelation of Itself through nature, history, and the human soul.

As stated earlier, in the ancient Near East names implied definite existence. People then believed that by their naming a particular thing it would become a reality (within their consciousness) for them.[32] The name implied a dimension of intimacy. By knowing an individual's name, one entered the personal realm of that individual. Thus, knowing the divine name brings one into an intimacy with that very divine presence.

---

[32]As an example, see Gen. 2:19–20a. God purposely brought to Adam all the animals so that he might name them. Thus, by naming the animals and the flying creatures, Adam was able to exert a measure of influence over them. This event is an expansion of the idea presented in Gen. 1:28.

EL SHADDAI

The name *el shaddai* was known to the Hebrew patriarchs.[33] It has been translated as "the Almighty," or "the Sufficient one." No Hebrew expert knows for certain the root meaning of this name of God.[34] Some suggest that its roots refer to the "mountain god"[35] and others that they refer to "the Breasted One," i.e., "the One who nourishes."

In an essay entitled "The God with Breasts: *el shaddai* in the Bible," Professor David Biale says: "Fertility notions are connected with the image of an androgenous god. . . . the possibility that God reflects the whole human condition — and not just His masculine aspect - was already evident to some biblical authors."[36]

JEHOVAH - YAHWEH

Before concluding our discussion of *yahweh*, let's consider the name "Jehovah" which derives from *yhwh*. The

---

[33]See Ex. 6:4.

[34]As of today there are no convincing traditions concerning its meaning. There is no way one can support and vindicate the translation as "God Almighty." *Shaddai* is of great antiquity, and this explains the difficulty in ascertaining its meaning. In Aramaic it means "Strong One." The traditional rendering in English, "Almighty," derives from the Latin Vulgate "Omnipotent."

[35]Modern interpreters connect *shaddai* with the Akkadian term *shadu*, "mountain," a royal and divine appellation: "The One of the mountain." However this is pure conjecture.

[36]See footnote 16 of this chapter concerning feminine roles attributed to *yahweh*.

name "Jehovah" came about through a transcription error by a medieval Christian scholar, Petrus Galatinus. He was confessor to Pope Leo X, around 1518 C.E. Galatinus transliterated *yhwh* into the Latin consonants *jhvh* and combined the vocalization (vowels) of the Hebrew term *adonai* (Lord) with these Latin consonants, producing the name "Jehovah."

The Hebrews considered the term *yahweh* so sacred that they never pronounced it. Biblical scribes substituted *adonai* (Lord) every time they read *yhwh*.

CONCLUSION

Besides the technical meaning of the term "God" or even a discussion of the aspects of God, if one were to ask a devout Easterner what God means to him, he would not reply in theological or philological terms. He would be more direct and simply respond, "God is my breath, my heartbeat and my life." To the devout consciousness of a Near Easterner, the living God encompasses him or her and watches over them as a shepherd watches over his flock. The song of the poetic psalmist describes this awareness of, and sensitivity to, God very clearly.

As the hart pants after the waterbrook
so pants my being after you,
O *Yahweh*![37]

---

[37]The Aramaic text actually uses *mariyah* — "Lord." However, I employed the Hebrew text here in my translation. It uses *yhwh* - *Yahweh*, the name of Israel's God. Some scholars suggest that the Aramaic term *mariyah* derives from two Aramaic words: *mar* ("Lord") and the abbreviated

Thirsting for you is my being,
O living God!
When shall I come to see your face?. . .
Deep cries out to deep
at the sound of your waterfalls.[38]

O *Yahweh*,
You have thoroughly examined me and known me.
You know how I conduct my life.[39]
You have discerned my thoughts from on high.
You know my way and my paths,
You have closely followed all my ways.
If there is any change in my speech,
O *Yahweh*,
You know it completely,
from the first to the very last.
You have formed me
and placed your hand upon me.
For me, such knowledge is too wonderful!
It is powerful!
I cannot master such power!
Where shall I go from Your spirit?
Or to where shall I flee from Your presence?
If I ascend into the heavens,
You are there

---

form of the name of *yahweh* ("yah"). Thus, in Aramaic the term *mariyah* may have originally meant "Lord Yah."

[38]Ps. 42:1–2, 7, Aramaic Peshitta Text, Errico translation.

[39]Literally it reads: "You know my sitting down and my rising up." This is a Semitic idiom and refers to one's conduct and behavior.

If I descend into Sheol,[40]
behold, You are there also.
If I lift up my wings like those of an eagle,
and dwell in the far-out parts of the sea,
Even there shall your hand lead me,
and your right hand shall hold me.[41]

---

[40]*Sheol* is the most common word used in Hebrew Scripture to refer to the abode of the dead. It occurs about 66 times in the Bible.

[41]Ps. 139:1–10, Aramaic Peshitta Text, Errico translation. The Aramaic Bible numbers this psalm as 138 instead of 139.

PART TWO

The Creation Story

It is true that the ancient Hebrews, unlike the Greeks, evinced no outstanding talent for scientific thought. Yet incredibly, it was Genesis rather than the Greek philosophers and scientists that arrived at the concept of a "uni-verse" created by one will and hence governed by universal laws of nature.

——————— Robert Gordis

Chapter 4

THE MYSTERIES OF CREATION

CREATION

There was movement.
Mysterious, compassionate
winds
slowly, gently
caressed the chaotic mass.
The depths were stirred!
There was light! There was darkness! There was sky!
The earth was born!
Movement was everywhere.

Sound was heard.
The soil moved. The ground heaved.
The mountains peaked.
There was life! There was green!
The plants came out from hiding.
The earth groaned. The trees stood.
Movement was everywhere.

Life was felt.
The air was turbulent. Flight was in motion.
The waters were disturbed. The sea was crowded.
Images were seen. The forms were dense.
Earth felt their weight.
Movement was everywhere.

Secrets were opened.
There was heat! There was passion!
The earth trembled. The sky wept.
There was man! There was woman!
Movement was everywhere.

There was rest.
The cosmos glowed. The stars embraced.
There was order. There was intelligence.
There was peace.
God was everywhere![1]

THE BEGINNING
GENESIS 1:1

In the beginning God created the heavens and the earth.

The Aramaic and Hebrew term *brsheeth*, "in-the-beginning," is a problem not only for the modern reader but for scholars as well. Should it be translated as "In the beginning" or "When God began to create"? Most biblical experts constantly debate the entire opening verse because one has to decide whether the verse is a principal clause or a subordinate temporal phrase. In other words, it is a question of knowing which is the proper Hebrew syntax.

Beside the above-mentioned difficulty, verse 1 presents the reader with another challenge. Philosophically and theologically, one might ask the following questions: "How can there be

---

[1]Rocco A. Errico, *Creation: A Poem*. San Antonio: Aramaic Bible Center, 1976, Costa Mesa: Noohra Foundation, 1986.

72

a beginning?" "Did something come from nothing?" "Was there a time when God didn't know He was going to create a universe?" And the problem increases if we explore the idea further and ask, "Did a new idea suddenly occur in the Omniscient Mind?" "How is that possible?" If it did, then there was a time when God did not know. Then, "How can *elohim* be omniscient?"

There are literally volumes of writings, dissertations and debates arguing the various interpretations of "In the beginning." One school of translators rejects the traditional phrase "In the beginning." They prefer to translate it as "When God began to create." This translation is similar to *Enuma Elish*, "When on High." Nonetheless, many biblical authorities claim that the traditional way of translating the first phrase as "In the beginning" clearly suggests that God had created the universe out of nothing.

Then again, other biblical scholars believe that Genesis 1:2 hints that some sort of primordial substance existed from the beginning, and that this substance provided the raw material for creation. Therefore these scholars propose the idea that God did not create the universe out of nothing. Today, after extensive scholastic argument[2] and grammatical discussion, it has been shown that verse 1 is a principal clause which was prefixed to the cosmological narrative.[3] To quote U. Cassuto, " . . . the first verse is an independent sentence that constitutes a formal introduction to the entire section, and expresses at the outset, with majestic brevity, the main thought of the section:

---

[2]For a scholarly and comprehensive account of the arguments concerning Gen. 1:1, see Claus Westermann, *Genesis 1–11: A Commentary*, pp. 94–97.

[3]Nonetheless there is still disagreement.

73

that in the beginning . . . the remotest past that the human mind can conceive, God created the heavens and the earth."[4]

Verse one echoes a hymn of praise to the creator of heaven and earth. We now know that there is nothing in the cosmogonies of Israel's Near Eastern neighbors that is comparable to the introductory phrase of the *torah* creation account. Genesis 1:1 is totally original.

The author's intent is not to pinpoint a precise moment in time. For him it is God's creative act that counts. It is helpful to understand that (a) he is not stating or hinting that God created the universe out of nothing, and (b) he is not suggesting that God took preexisting primordial substance and created the universe. These two very distinct ideas were not present during the author's day but belonged to another era of philosophical thought and inquiry. Greek thought was not prevalent in Israel then and could not have influenced the creation narrator.[5]

We must also realize that the writer was not familiar with our Western theological, scientific, or philosophical questions and approaches. He did not learn our sciences nor was he nurtured in our modern cultures. His emphasis is simply that God is the creator of heaven and earth. The purpose of the creation poem was to bring God into relationship with everything, from the stars of the heavens to the smallest insects on earth and, of course, into relationship with humanity.

---

[4]Umberto Cassuto, *A Commentary on the Book of Genesis: Part One, From Adam to Noah*, p. 20.

[5]The two above notions were of Greek origin and philosophical thought. They were not a part of Semitic thought. Israel was affected by these Hellenistic ideas only late in its religious history. The Genesis creation account predates this particular Greek influence.

"In the beginning" implies that the primeval event is truly timeless and measureless. It is a state in which time does not exist. Heaven and earth are the creative acts of *elohim*, the transcendent Deity.

THE SEMITIC TERM "CREATED"

The Aramaic and Hebrew verb "created" *bra* (*bara*) is an ancient Semitic word to which the writer gives the special theological sense of *creation by God alone*. It is God only who has created the awesome universe. In other words, by recognizing God as creator we are to respect the beauty and sacredness of the heavens and the earth. For the heavens and the earth are God's handiwork. Poetically, God constructed the earth as His sanctuary and the heavens as its ceiling (dome). His mysterious presence permeates His glorious temple.

CAUSALITY

The Aramaic term *ithea*, "self-existent" or "essence," is another name for God.[6] *Ithea*, or "God," transcends all creations and, in quality, is the essence of life and the foundation of order. Thus we may also think of God as the "Absolute." According to the Genesis narrative, all things are created by God, exist, and are made manifest. Everything subsists in essence, and nothing exists without essence. The universe and humankind are manifestations of God and reflections of that Essence.

---

[6]See Chapter 3, subheading "The Term 'God.'"

75

The creator and his creative manifestations are inseparable and holistically one. By this statement, I do not suggest
or hint at the doctrine of monism, which blurs the distinction
between the various grades of being. The infinite always
embraces the finite. It manifests "creations" by becoming finite
without ever losing its infinite Self. The principle is: God is
unity in diversity. To help illustrate this idea, let us consider
the physical form. Human feet are uniquely distinct from the
head, and yet the head and the feet are inseparable. In other
words, the human body is a diversified unity.

I also wish to make it clear that I do not refer to any
subtle form of pantheism. *Elohim* is not at all like the gods and
goddesses of the Mesopotamian myths.[7] There is a big difference between the Genesis transcendent creator and the
immanent creator gods of the Near Eastern stories. Not only
were the deities of Chaldea immanent but they were an integral
part of the natural order that they were supposed to control.
For instance, in the Babylonian myth *Enuma Elish,* Apsu was a
male deity and Tiamat a female deity. Apsu and Tiamat were
personifications of a primeval watery "chaos." They were the
ones who "begot" and "gave birth" to other deities. There is no
idea of transcendence in this myth. On the other hand, the

---

[7]Myths were dramatic, sacred stories that legalized the permanency of
ancient institutions, customs, rites, and beliefs in the area where they were
active. They also served to approve any changes in the customs, rites, and
beliefs. Our English word *myth* is derived from the Greek term *muthos,*
meaning "word," "speech," "the thing spoken," or "the tale told." Mythology
is a Greek concept. Myth has always functioned as a succinct validation of
puzzling laws, rites, and social customs.

Genesis creation saga emphasizes God's transcendence and incomparableness.[8]

It may be difficult to think in terms of a self-existent principle, such as God as wholeness, eternity as timeless, and infinity as spaceless and sizeless. A self-existent principle is not a cause. It simply is, and that is all there is.

In the relative world, it appears that there is causality. We constantly observe events as separate occurrences, but in reality there are no separate events. According to modern physics, the entire universe moves and creates uniformly and inseparably. It teaches us that nothing acts separately from, or independent of, anything else. Besides the above, quantum physics also instructs us that at subatomic levels there is no cause and effect.[9]

PHILOSOPHICAL CAUSALITY

Common paradigms of thinking have chopped the world in two; we think of ourselves as the subject and the world as an object. In other words, the world has become an object of our minds. Because of this phenomenon, we perceive ourselves as separate from the world and view daily occurrences in piece-meal fashion. Therefore we think and speak of events and objects as separate from and independent of each other. This is because our selective perception focuses on what appears to be an isolated aspect of reality, including ourselves. This is just

---

[8]For the incomparableness of God, see Isa. 40:25–26, 42:5, 8–9; Ps. 89:6, 12.

[9]See Fred Alan Wolf, *Taking the Quantum Leap: The New Physics for Nonscientists.*

one reason why events appear to us as caused. Nonetheless, the actuality is that there is only one holistic happening.[10]

There are certain philosophies, metaphysical assumptions and religious dogma that portray God as "First Cause." But this is not the thought of the creation account. The author is not writing of a "first cause." In Western history the notion that God is "First Cause" was originally proclaimed by Plato and Aristotle[11] and expanded by Thomas Aquinas. This notion reached its zenith in the eighteenth century as the major cosmological argument for the existence of God.[12]

Between the late 1960s and early 1970s, from time to time the late Dr. George M. Lamsa and I would engage in lengthy discussions about God as "First Cause." One day, he was kind enough to impart information for me to use during my research work on the idea of God and causality. The following is that material (my notes) in its original form.[13] The words in brackets are my insertions.

> God is not first cause as some philosophers and metaphy-
> sicians think He is. For what is born of a cause is not
> eternal [absolute, infinite] but is subjective [relative, finite].
> God is eternal [timeless] and self-existent. He always was
> and shall be forever and ever. There was no time when He
> did not exist and was not manifested in the universe.

---

[10]See Abraham J. Heschel, *Man is not Alone: A Philosophy of Religion*, "The World as an Object," pp. 38–40.

[11]According to Near Eastern history, the Persians were the first to proclaim God as "First Cause."

[12]For a thorough scientific presentation of "first cause," see Paul Davies, *God and the New Physics*, pp. 25–43, "Did God Create the Universe?"

[13]My notes of the teachings of my late mentor, Dr. Lamsa, whom I affectionately called in Aramaic "rabbi," have never been published.

Moreover, the sun, moon, and stars depend on Him [on the self-existent principle] for their existence. They exist to serve. This is because they derive their power from God to serve His creations.

God's existence cannot be due to a cause. If it were, then God would have to come into existence through circumstances. And it would prove that there was a time when He did not exist. Moreover, the cause would be greater than God. A cause is not an essence. God's existence and His attributes were revealed to man in the fullness of time. But, that which is revealed has no beginning. Since ideas are born in the fullness of time, they seem to have a beginning, but in reality, are eternal [timeless]. ... On the other hand, that which is eternal [timeless] and changeless, cannot be comprehended by that which is caught in time, therefore changeable.

Moreover, a substance or an essence cannot be defined nor attributed to a cause. Thus, if God, or the universe, was the result of a cause, then what produced the cause? And, if God were the result of a cause, then God would have no intelligence and the cause would be greater than God. Then God would have derived His existence from the cause.[14]

Dr. Lamsa concludes his thoughts with this idea:

For as a cause is the result of an effect, so an effect is the result of a cause. I believe a tree produces a seed of its own kind, and a hen produces an egg because there must be a pattern first to reproduce itself.

---

[14]See Ernest S. Holmes, *Your Invisible Power*, pp. 58–59: "Truth has no cause and ... there is no effect external to It."

COMPLEMENTARY UNIVERSE

Modern physicists refer to the cosmos as a "self-creating universe." Thomas Berry, a theologian who is known as a "geologian," refers to the earth as a "self-regulating organism." According to the theory of quantum physics, the universe burst forth into existence spontaneously. Life itself acts instantaneously, simultaneously and spontaneously.

The Second Law of Thermodynamics says that energy cannot be created or lost. It can only be transmuted into other forms of energy. During transmutation of energy from one form to another, no power is lost. In the entire universe nothing is the effect of something else.

The late Zen master, Dr. D.T. Suzuki, used to say, "form is formlessness and formlessness is form." The noted physicist W. Heisenberg, who received the Nobel prize for his theory on the "Uncertainty Principle," scientifically explains the creation of the universe based on the "Uncertainty Principle"[15] and not on "Cause and Effect."

In the scientific world there are physicists who argue that matter came first and produced consciousness, while other scientists hold that consciousness came first and produced matter. On the other hand, there are materialistic philosophers who deny the existence of Mind, while others, opposing this perception, perceive the physical universe (matter) as unreal. And what is most interesting is the fact that the ancient

---

[15]See Werner Heisenberg, *Physics and Beyond*. My work is not an attempt to present or prove any scientific theory of creation. It is my intention to stimulate the reader to inquire further on the subject matter. I highly recommend Paul Davies, *The Mind of God: The Scientific Basis for a Rational World*, for a fuller scientific presentation. See Bibliography.

Chinese, being free of Western thought, did not think in "Either/Or" terms. Oriental philosophy teaches that everything arose mutually. Matter does not precede consciousness, nor does consciousness precede matter, but both are complementary to each other. Once we move beyond "Either/Or" forms of thinking, we can realize and discern the cosmos in its complementary form.

To further illustrate this idea, let us take the notion of something and nothing. In reality, something and nothing complement each other. We cannot have something without nothing. We may also consider the idea of so-called space and objects. Space, as it appears to us, with its relative distance between objects, enables objects to stand out. On the other hand, objects give a dimension to space.[16] As the reader can see, it is difficult to maintain fixed ideas and notions in a complex, dynamic, and ever-changing world of science.[17]

I shall repeat some ideas that I have discussed in this chapter. Let us recall that the term "beginning," to the Eastern author, puts emphasis on God's creative acts. It does not connote "a beginning" as we might attempt to understand it. Nor is the Semitic writer depicting God as "First Cause." To him the universe was not caused, but created, by God. The universe is a constant happening — continual, endless creating. It is like a tree perpetually bearing fruit because of God's creative act.

---

[16]See Fred Alan Wolf, *Taking the Quantum Leap*, "The Act of Creation: Observation," and "The Paradoxical Cube," pp. 127–32.

[17]Those readers who wish to explore the subjects of causality and the Principle of Complementarity, I refer to the Bibliography for additional study sources.

GOD

The term "God" — *elohim* — in the creation account would not have the same meaning for the author as it does for us in the modern Western world. We would ask a multitude of questions.[18] For the author of the Genesis account, God as creator acts and speaks the creative word. God is not the object of his thought to be studied and scrutinized. God is the very act and word itself. In Semitic thought a man, his word, and acts (deeds) are all one. An individual's utterance represents him and his own energy. "In the beginning was the word and that word was always with God and God was always that word."[19] In other words, the writer understands *elohim* to be all that he describes about Him, the creator of heaven and earth.

As for the Semitic word *elohim*, it was a common noun, and the Hebrew people used it to designate any deity or deities. So it not only means "God," but "gods," "the god," and "the gods." Its origin and history points way back in the history of Israel and to the land of Canaan.[20]   *Elohim* is a Hebrew variant of an ancient Semitic term for one god of many. For instance, the Assyrians and Chaldeans used *ilu*; among the Hittites and in the Ugaritic texts, *el*; among the South Arabians *il*. *El* was the chief god of the Phoenician pantheon and is often mentioned in Ugaritic poems dating from the 14th century

---

[18]Such existential questions as: "Does a god exist?" "Why and how does a god exist?" "Is a god necessary?" "Who and what is this god?" "Is this creator-deity 'first Cause?'"   These ideas would not concern the biblical author.

[19]Jn. 1:1, Aramaic Peshitta Text, Errico translation.

[20]See Chapter 3, subheading "The Term 'God.'"

B.C.E. The word *elohim* moved through many stages of meaning. In Gen. 1 the meaning would belong to the latest stage of development: *elohim*, the unequivocal God, the one and only Creator of the universe and human family, Ruler of nature, Source of life.

Hebrew sages also used the term *elohim* when they wished to imply God as transpersonal, an abstraction, or transcendental. They also connected the name with ethics, law, and justice. Usually, *elohim* simply expresses the idea of deity without being specific. However, there are times when Jewish scribes specified *yahweh* as God.[21] For instance, "the Lord, he is God," i.e., "*yahweh*, he is *elohim*." The Semitic name *Elijah* connotes the same meaning "my God is *yahweh*."

HEAVEN AND EARTH

The dualistic term "heaven and earth" is a common phrase throughout Genesis and the entire Bible. Hebrew scribes employ it to mean totality. Scriptures generally use two words of the same meaning or two opposites to show totality. In this verse, it expresses the idea of the cosmic phenomena.

Before continuing, let us understand what the first three verses of Genesis say to us. Gen. 1:1 clearly states that God created everything. It serves as an introduction and tells it all. Our study of the text could end with the first verse. However, the writer continues his narrative. Surprisingly, Gen. 1:2 does not inform us about the creative process. The second verse only describes the circumstances in which God's action is going

---

[21]See Cassutto, *The Documentary Hypothesis*, Chapters Two and Three, "Divine Names and More about the Divine Names," pp. 15–41.

to take place. It is Gen. 1:3 that begins the descriptive creative procedure.

THE SITUATION
GENESIS 1:2

Now the earth was chaos and darkness was upon the deep. But the spirit of God hovered compassionately (moved gently) over the surface of the waters.

THE SCENE

The picture before us is a scene of overpowering darkness, watery mass, and chaos. We are told that the earth is in a state of unformed, primitive matter. All raw material and forces are present but latent. Darkness prevails. But, simultaneously, an energized life-force sweeps over the surface of the primeval ocean. The divine presence has the situation in hand and is about to begin its work. Let us now examine the key Semitic descriptive terms in verse 2.

CHAOTIC EARTH

The first term is "chaos." Scripture says: "As for the earth, it was chaos." The peculiar two-word phrase *tohu wa-bohu* (Hebrew) or *toh w-boh* (Aramaic) simply mean "chaos." There have been many attempts to connect these two words with an ancient mythical background. Some researchers have sought to prove that *bohu* comes from the Sumerian-Babylonian

84

goddess *Bau* or from the Phoenician goddess *Baau*. These arguments are no longer tenable. *Tohu wa-bohu* are two Semitic nouns expressing one idea — chaos. Since the earth was in chaos, there could be no meaning for its existence just yet. This description of chaos, darkness, and the deep was very frightening for the Israelites.

However, one biblical commentator suggests that the primordial state merely represented God's preparatory work. "Just as the potter, when he wishes to fashion a beautiful vessel, takes first of all a lump of clay, and places it upon his wheel in order to mould it according to his wish, so the creator first prepared for himself the raw material of the universe."[22]

The second term is the "deep." Both the Hebrew word *t-hom* and the Aramaic term *t-homa* are translated as "the deep," but they mean the primeval ocean. This massive ocean of water was everywhere. Gen. 1:2 does not present "the deep" as a divinity. In the Mesopotamian story the waters are represented by a goddess. The entire Hebrew account is bereft of supernatural deities and powers in the natural elements. This is a pure, monotheistic account of creation.

THE HOVERING COMPASSIONATE SPIRIT

Unrelenting chaos, incessant darkness, and unbounded waters were the evils, fears, and horrors of the ancient Near East. Verse two depicts a stark and foreboding picture of all these elements at the beginning of God's creative works. The author makes a startling contrast between these feared forces and God's creative presence. Everything is excessively dark.

---

[22]Cassutto, *A Commentary on the Book of Genesis: Part One*, p. 23.

Matter is in a state of meaningless form. God's life-giving, creative, and sustaining power hovers over the primeval ocean. The creator's dynamic spirit symbolizes motion — the basic element for change. It also symbolizes the opposite principle of desolation embodied in the darkness and the deep.

"Hovered" is the third term. It comes from the Hebrew *mrahpeth* and the Aramaic *mrahpa*. The Semitic root *mrp* means "to flutter" or "to shake". This form of the verb does not have the sense of "brooding." It implies motion, a gentle movement. The word also means "to hover tremulously." However, there is something more to consider. In Aramaic *mrahpa* in its root also means "to pity," "to cherish," and "to have compassion." God, like a parent, hovered compassionately over the chaotic mass. This was earth's assurance of meaningful existence and future development.

DARKNESS

The author does not tell us anything about the origin of darkness. Nor does he inform us that God explicitly created it. Nevertheless, verse 1 implies that God created darkness because He created everything. Isaiah the prophet clearly attributes the existence of darkness to divine creation.[23] We, on the other hand, usually attribute darkness to nothing more than the absence of light.

Darkness is a mystery. Ancient sages symbolized darkness as an evil, horror, and terror. Modern thinkers continue to depict darkness and the color black as evil, sorrow, disaster, distress, ignorance, blindness, superstition, and lack of

---

[23]See Isa. 45:7.

truth. This is based solely on a relative, one-sided point of view.

There are no natural universal forces that are maleficent in and of themselves. Positive and negative forces create phenomena, and both are necessary. Darkness and blackness have another side, which we seldom realize. The following is a poem which I wrote in 1972 about the uniqueness of darkness:

In the darkness of the womb,
life is conceived.
In the darkness of the soil,
seeds germinate.
In the darkness of the inner mind,
ideas are born.
Darkness is nature's time of rest,
formation, incubation,
rejuvenation, and secret rendezvous
of invisible powers
and unseen realities.

We also teach that only light and the color white are symbolic of God. But darkness and the color black are also representations of God. Darkness, as a metaphor, presents God as the Inscrutable Source, the Unknowable and the Unmanifest. According to the early Egyptian writers, the first principle is characterized as darkness because it is beyond all classified and rational conceptions.

In Chinese philosophy darkness and the color black represent the Yin Principle, the feminine energy. This feminine principle is creative, hidden, negative receptivity. It is not passive, but responsive to active, positive forces. In electricity the negative pole is the receptive feminine force. Thinking superficially, we equate a negative force with an evil power. This is not so. It is from the creative feminine womb (dark, negative force) that all life is generated. And it is from this womb that all life springs.

Metaphorically, the divine is also feminine in that it is a mystery. For me, the use of gender in describing God is strictly metaphorical. It helps us, at least partially, to understand and relate to the mystery of God. On the other hand, biblical writers depict God in the masculine gender, but not as opposed to the feminine gender. Misogyny is not a part of biblical writings.

In certain instances biblical writers refer to darkness in a higher, more positive mode. God is often depicted as surrounded by darkness, clouds, and tempests. "And *yahweh* said to Moses, behold, I am coming to you in a thick [dark, black] cloud . . . And it happened on the third day in the morning that there were thunders and lightnings and a thick cloud . . . "[24] The song of David confirms the idea that God's dwelling place was in darkness. He poetically and figuratively says, "He [God] made darkness his secret shelter. His tent round about him was darkness of waters and thick clouds of the sky."[25]

In the ancient days darkness was "the mystery of all mysteries." It was only natural, then, that God was represented as dwelling in, and being surrounded by, darkness. Life is God, the Inscrutable Source. Life is a bittersweet mystery that is lived, but never fully solved.

---

[24] Ex. 19:9a, 16b, Aramaic Peshitta Text, Errico translation.
[25] 2 Sam. 22:12, Aramaic Peshitta Text, Errico translation.

We are now ready to move into the next phase of the creation narrative. Let us review the second verse. It leads us directly into the scene where God's creative actions begin:

The entire scene vibrates with the compassionate, empathetic Presence of divine love and intelligence. There is chaos and water everywhere. God moves and creates in the midst of the dreadful and dominant inky blackness. . . . *w-mar alaha: nehwey noohra. . . . Then God exclaimed: Let there be Light!*

Chapter 5

THE CREATION PROCESS

DIVINE ORDER BEGINS
GENESIS 1:3-5

Then God exclaimed: Let there be light! And there was light. Now God saw the light that it was beautiful. So God separated the light from the darkness. Then God named the light: Day. And He named the darkness: Night. Now it was evening, then it was morning, day one.

THE COMMANDING WORD

"Then God exclaimed: Let there be light! . . ." It is at this point that the author begins his description of the creation process. Ancients believed that creation came into existence through various methods.[1] One method was creating through utterance (command), such as we find in the biblical narrative.

The creative "word" idea also appears in a Memphite Egyptian cosmogony.[2] Ptah, the most high god of Memphis, created everything by his word ("heart and tongue"). Though this extant account is dated 700 B.C.E., it derives from an original text dating from two thousand years earlier. The "word" was the activating power of Ptah's thoughts. His "heart"

---

[1]See Chapter 1 subheading "The Ancient Near East."

[2]See James B. Pritchard, *Ancient Near Eastern Texts*, 3rd ed., "The Theology of Memphis," pp. 4-6.

(mind) represented thought, and his "tongue" (word) was the symbol of command, or power.

SEMITIC THOUGHT

"A man is valued by his words" is an age-old Near Eastern Aramaic proverb. According to Semitic thinking, an individual's utterance carries with it his/her vital energy and essence. The uttered word is a very mysterious and powerful force. Easterners believe that once a word is spoken, it immediately acts. This is the reason we find so much admonition against idle words in Scripture. God's creative command is the same as a deed. His utterance is a projection of His creative energy. The inference in the scriptures quoted above (Gen. 1:3–5) is that God made the light and called it into existence.

LIGHT

The science of physics instructs us that matter is nothing more than gravitationally trapped light or energy. *Noohra*, in Aramaic, means "light," "sight," "insight," "brightness," "brilliance," "enlightenment," and "understanding." Light is the essence of all substance. Everything in the universe is reducible to light. All matter, before manifesting in particular forms such as trees, plants, etc., is pure light. Present in all form is a hidden pattern. This pattern is its own light, which will eventually come forth in its own distinctive shape.

MODERN SCIENCE

Modern cosmology has established that the primeval fireball was the beginning of the universe. This fireball suddenly appeared. All existing matter and energy are a direct result of the appearance of "light," i.e., the primeval fireball. Dr. Nathan Aviezer, Professor and Chairperson of Physics at Bar-Ilan University, Israel, also says:

> The big bang theory explains that the universe originally consisted of a mixture of a plasma and the light of the primeval fireball. At that time, the universe appeared *dark* because of the plasma. The sudden transformation of the plasma into atoms shortly after the creation caused the electromagnetic radiation ("light") of the primeval fireball to "separate" from the previously dark universe and shine freely throughout space. This separation is called decoupling in scientific terminology.[3]

THE BIBLICAL IDEA OF LIGHT

Darkness was suddenly energized and flooded with brightness. The creator spoke the word of command and light presented itself. Light was necessary so that the creative work could be divided into time. In other words, temporal creation preceded spatial work.

> The first three acts of creation are not as it were the manufacture of substances, but the basic divisions of the

---

[3]Nathan Aviezer, *In the Beginning: Biblical Creation and Science*, p. 16. For a complete, modern, scientific explanation of creation and the biblical creation, I recommend this book. See Bibliography for more details.

universe. Separation of light from darkness is temporal, not spatial. The creation of light is put before these divisions because it renders possible the temporal succession into which the world is set. . . . God creates brightness and thereby makes possible the basic cycle of time and order.[4]

Again, I remind the reader that this account is a literary structure and not a literal depiction of creation. The author reworked ancient traditional creation motifs and divided them into seven days. Let us recall that the number seven represents perfection and completion.[5]

THE LITERARY PATTERN

Day One

Light, the division
of light and darkness
into day and night.

Day Four

Sun, moon, stars and their
responsibilities to govern
the seasons, years, and days.

Day Two

Firmament (sky), the
division of the waters
above and below the
firmament.

Day Five

Waters teeming with swarms
of living creatures, flying
creatures in the expanse of
of the firmament (sky).

---

[4]Claus Westermann, *Genesis 1–11: A Commentary*, p. 112.
[5]See Chapter 1 subheading "The Number Seven."

<u>Day Three</u>	<u>Day Six</u>
The appearance of the dry land, vegetation, and herb-yielding seed and fruit-bearing trees.	Land creatures, i.e., animals, reptiles, wild land beasts, and humankind.

The seventh day is the climax of the first and second sets of three days each. A unique teaching method and parallelism are involved in the use of six days, as illustrated above and explained below.

SIX DAYS

Parallelism in Semitic writing is very important. In the creation account, days four through six correspond with days one through three: (1) Days one and four with the creation of light, night, day, sun, moon, and stars, all conform as if they were one unit. (2) Days two and five, with the creation of the firmament, divisions of waters, fish of the sea, flying creatures of the sky, also belong together as one unit. (3) Days three and six, with the appearance of dry land, vegetation, herb yielding seed, fruit-bearing trees, animals, reptiles, wild land beasts, and humankind, are as one occurrence also.

If we read the six days as literal workdays we distort the scheme of the creation epic. The narrator depicts one complete grand happening divided into six creative units and one unit for repose. Let us realize that the author was not present to see God creating the heavens and the earth.

The seventh and final day is a time of rest. God rests, not because He feels debilitated, but because He has completed His creative work. Humanly speaking, God is satisfied and

95

content with creation. In the Psalms the songwriter poetically chants: "The universe declares the glory of God and the firmament manifests the work of his hands. Day after day pours out speech and night after night reveals understanding."[6]

The use of six creation days is a literary device and not an actual detailed description of creation. One needs to read and understand the narrative as a whole. Although we can explain the creation story today with modern science, all of that is immaterial. In this story the dominant point is "God created the heavens and the earth." There are, of course, many subordinate and other salient points to the creation account. Nevertheless, the most important theme is that *elohim* is creator.

THE APPEARANCE OF LIGHT

Light is usually the first creative act described in early Mesopotamian cosmologies. For instance, in the Egyptian cosmogony of Hermopolis, light appears immediately after chaos. The biblical creation account also follows this order making light primary. However, there is one major difference between these accounts. Light is divine in the Egyptian epic. It is Ra or Re who shines over the primeval chaos. In Genesis 1, light is not a divinity. It is simply a creation of God.

There may also be another reason for light appearing as the first creative act. Pristine societies unpretentiously reasoned and observed that brightness (light) always came before the appearance of the sun. In other words, light (brightness) acted as a herald of its coming source.

---

[6]See Ps. 19:1–2, Aramaic Peshitta Text, Errico translation.

According to Chinese philosophy, light and the color white represent the Yang Principle — the masculine energy. This masculine principle is creative, open, positive activity. In electricity, the positive pole is the active [masculine] force. According to Scripture, "light" is also symbolic of life, joy, justice and deliverance.[7] Scripture also tells us that God robes Himself with light: "You cover yourself with light like a mantle."[8]

GOOD OR BEAUTIFUL?

"And God saw the light, that it was good."[9] In the English version of the Hebrew text, this phrase is now translated as "God saw how good the light was. . . . " *Tov* in Hebrew means "good." However, the Peshitta Aramaic text uses the term *shapeera* (shapira) throughout the narrative. This Aramaic word primarily means "beautiful" and secondarily "good." In Aramaic the equivalent term for the Hebrew *tov*, "good," is *tawa*. But the Peshitta text does not use *tawa*. It uses *shapeera*.

Why is this? *Tov* "good" embraces three implications: (1) an aesthetic quality, (2) a moral quality, and (3) "good" in the sense of function and purpose. Knowing this, one may translate the word *tov* as "lovely," "pleasing," or "beautiful." This is exactly what the translators of the Hebrew text into the Aramaic language did with the word *tov*. They used *shapeera*, "beautiful." "Now God saw the light that it was beautiful."

---

[7]See Ps. 49:20; 56:14; Job 30:26; Ps. 97:11; Isa. 9:1; Ps 27:1.

[8]Ps. 104:2, Aramaic Peshitta Text, Errico translation.

[9]Gen. 1:4a, King James Version.

Seven times God saw how pleasing and beautiful everything was.[10] He was so deeply impressed with the six days of creation that the writer has God seeing everything as overwhelmingly good and beautiful: "Now, behold, how exceedingly beautiful it was!"[11]

However, despite the above interpretation, a few biblical commentators believe that in these passages the word *tov* implies a moral quality. They hold that from this point in the narrative evil is to be understood on a moral rather than a mythological level.[12] In other words, the Hebrew writer completely nullifies the ancient notion of inherent primordial evil in creation. And according to him, all creation is inherently good because God created it.

DARKNESS COMES TO LIGHT

Scripture says God saw that the light was good. It does not say that darkness was good. There is a reason for this idea. Darkness was out of balance. It was incessant and unrelenting in its hold on the universe. A chaotic earth and unbounded waters were under the power of total darkness. The sudden appearance of light broke its tenacious grip. Then *elohim* immediately perceived the goodness of light. Nonetheless, the reader must realize that it is the narrator who places the judgment value on light and not God.

-----

[10]See Gen 1:4, 10, 12, 18, 21, 25, 31.

[11]Gen. 1:31, Aramaic Peshitta Text, Errico translation.

[12]See Nahum M. Sarna, *Genesis: The JPS Torah Commentary.*

LIGHT AND DARKNESS BALANCE EACH OTHER

The creation of light was not intended to dispel darkness. It was needed to balance it. Brightness came flooding in upon the darkness of the primeval chaos. The cycle of time began as the two entities turned into day and night, complementing each other in succession. God separating (differentiating) light from darkness brings into creation the pulse and movement of time.

Light was beautiful because it balanced the totality of darkness. On the other hand, too much light can be just as harmful as too much darkness. For instance, unrelenting sunshine creates a parched, barren desert. Light also needs to be balanced by darkness. When opposites balance, joy emerges.

NAMING — A CREATIVE ACT

Naming is extremely important in the Near East. Primitive Mesopotamian people equated namelessness with nonexistence. One Egyptian creation narrative depicts precreation as an era of namelessness - "When no name of anything had yet been named." In Chaldea (Babylon) the *Enuma Elish* depicts chaos as a time of namelessness in heaven and earth. Therefore, naming becomes a creative act initiating order and differentiation. Since naming is a creative act, the one who gives a name has power. In the Eden story when Adam named the animals, it showed he had authority over them.

Throughout the creation narrative God not only names light and darkness as "day" and "night," but the firmament as "sky," the dry land as "earth," and the collection of waters as "seas." This way the writer expresses God's absolute sovereignty over heaven and earth and over the temporal and the spatial.

EVENING AND MORNING

"Day one" and "evening and morning" are poetic terms and phrases. The writer dramatizes God's creative activities in six scenes. He makes use of "evening and morning" and "day one . . . two . . . three . . . " and so forth, comparable to a curtain rising and falling between acts. Debates and disputes over the intent and meaning of "evening and morning" are unnecessary. They simply designate a closing and a beginning, and not a twenty-four-hour period. These expressions are further examples of metaphoric and symbolic language used to tell a primeval event. Interpreters debating the meaning of "evening and morning" only continue to misunderstand the intent of the text.

THE FIRMAMENT
GENESIS 1:6–8

Then God exclaimed: Let there be a firmament in the midst of the waters and let it separate the waters from the waters! So God made the firmament and separated the waters that are below the firmament from the waters that are above the firmament. And that is how it happened. Then God named the firmament: Sky. Now it was evening, then it was morning, day two.

The Aramaic and Hebrew word *raqia* means "expanse," "firmament," literally "beaten out," "stamped," "hammered out," "flattened," (as of metal). It suggests a thin, massive, transparent sheet stretched out to form a firm vault or dome over the earth.[13] Since the firmament acted as a transparent dividing wall to separate the waters, the early Hebrews attributed the blue color of the sky to the chaotic waters.[14] Job informs us that the firmament had pillars.[15] In 2 Sam. 22:8, the writer says that it also had foundations. However, the creation story does not say a word about pillars or foundations.

Among primitive peoples the idea that the heavens were solid was a widespread belief. This creation tradition of the firmament was handed down and followed in the Hebrew creation narrative. However, we must not think that this was a contemporary description of the world. This was part of the old tradition which the narrator had received and passed on.

Hebrew Scripture often refers to the primeval ocean (waters) which is above the solid vault of heaven. In the flood narrative, water pours down upon the earth through openings (windows) in the vault of heaven.[16] The book of the Revelation also mentions that heaven contains a crystal-clear mass of water known as "the sea of glass."[17]

When God names the firmament then it becomes known as the "sky" or the "heavens." Usually, the term "firmament" strictly refers to the celestial canopy (dome) that covers the earth. However, the term "heaven" has a broader meaning,

---

[13]Something like a bell, tent or roof. Ps. 104:2b says, ". . . Who spreads out the heavens like a tent," Aramaic Peshitta Text, Errico translation. Our English word *firmament* derives from the Latin *firmamentum,* carrying the idea of something solid.

[14]See Gen. 1:7, Deut. 5:8.

[15]Job 26:11.

[16]See Gen. 7:11–12; 2 Kings 7:2, 19.

[17]Rev. 4:6.

pointing to anything that is above the earth, including the firmament.

HEAVEN

According to many early Near Eastern myths, heaven emerged as a deity. The Egyptian myth tells us that when heaven separated from earth, the gods climbed up to heaven. Heaven was also populated with all classes of gods and goddesses. It was the domain for the various activities of these deities. For example, the gods fought and killed each other; goddesses resurrected certain male gods; they also plotted and schemed; heavenly counsels met and decided the fate of humans.

Genesis 1 plainly declares that heaven is a creation of God and nothing more. It becomes the place for the storehouses of the winds, the snow, and the hail.[18] The sun, moon, and stars inhabit the heavens. Heaven provides space for the winged creatures to fly. Clearly, the author does not work with a mythical idea of heaven.

The creation account does not present *elohim* creating the heavens as a dwelling place for Himself. On the other hand, there are scriptures that refer to the heavens as God's abode. It is poets, prophets, and other Israelite authors who say that the heavens were the habitation of God. These biblical sages used ancient myths and traditions to express their poetic, figurative and descriptive language about God. According to these writings, God is enthroned in heaven and meets with His heavenly court; He rides the clouds as one would ride a chariot; earth becomes His footstool, and He fills the heavens with his

---

[18]See Job 37:9; 38:22; Ps. 135:7; Jer. 10:13.

mercy and compassion. All these sayings and a multitude of similar ones are figures of speech.

When one considers the historical context of the creation account, the author has obviously and completely depopulated heaven. Heaven is no longer a domicile for any divinity or personage. In this account not even God, as the creator, deems it necessary to inhabit it. Nonetheless, it was difficult to keep heaven uninhabited. In many apocalyptic and apocryphal writings heaven becomes repopulated with angelic beings, certain holy men, and prophets.

Hebrew myths and pseudepigraphical literature promote the idea of multiple heavens. The most common is the notion of seven heavens. In the New Testament, it was the dwelling place of the Messiah who "came down from above." It also became the place for the departed. Heaven as an abode for the dead is an ancient idea. It became firmly established in Egypt. Many Near Eastern religions believed in a soul form of life which survived the grave. Heaven housed famous kings and queens, their relatives, and servants.

EARTH AND SEAS
GENESIS 1:9–10

Then God exclaimed: Let the waters that are under the sky come together into one place, and let dry land appear! And that is how it happened. Then God named the dry land: Earth. And He named the collection of waters: Seas. Now God saw that it was beautiful.

In the creation process there are three things that are not explicitly explained, i.e., the earth, the darkness, and the

103

deep (ocean or waters).[19] However, the introductory statement, Gen. 1:1, says that "God created the heavens and the earth."[20] See also Gen. 2:1. The implication here and in Gen. 2:1 is that God created everything — the earth, the darkness, and the deep — despite the fact that the author does not precisely tell their origins.

Following the division of the waters, the narrator tells us that God calls for the gathering of waters to form seas so that earth can make its appearance. He does not present us with a description of the earth. He presents the earth as "dry land," i.e., an expanse ready for habitation.

The Hebrew view of the earth was the same as that of their Near Eastern neighbors. Their poets and prophets describe earth as a flat expanse, seen in the shape of either a disk or a circle upon the primeval waters.[21] Or they perceive earth as an outstretched garment spanning the void.[22] References also exist that depict the earth as having four corners. Again, the narrator tells us nothing about the shape or dimensions of the earth.

---

[19]Modern scientists have several theories as to how the earth, the oceans, and the continents came into existence. No one really knows.

[20]According to our top physicists, the presently known laws of physics cannot describe the actual point of creation. "The instant of creation remains unexplained." So says Professor Alan Guth, Massachusetts Institute of Technology, and Professor Paul Steinhardt, University of Pennsylvania.

[21]See Job 26:10; Isa. 40:22; Prov. 8:27.

[22]See Job 26:7; 38:13.

LIVING EARTH AND PLANTS
GENESIS 1:11–13

Then God exclaimed: Let the earth sprout vegetation, the herb-yielding seed according to its nature, and the fruit tree that bears fruit that is implanted in itself according to its nature, upon the earth! And that is how it happened. So the earth sprouted vegetation, the herb-yielding seed according to its nature, and the fruit tree that bears fruit that is implanted in itself according to its nature. And God saw that it was beautiful. Now it was evening, then it was morning, day three.

Usually, in the old, traditional patterns of the Near East, the origin of plants is written as a separate narrative. Mesopotamian writers present the origins of human beings, heaven and earth, and vegetation in three distinct cosmogonies. The opposite occurs in the Genesis creation story. The Hebrew writer presents all three origins in one narrative.

As the cosmic drama continues, we quickly learn that the soil (earth) responds to the command to sprout vegetation: herb-yielding seed and trees bearing life-sustaining fruits. God as creator also gives power to the plants to reproduce on their own. "Let the earth bring forth" means "let what is within come out." The plants are in the soil, and it releases them according to God's command.

Here we have the repeated idea of separation that follows the basic creation pattern. Vegetation is classified into two basic categories. Again, the narrator changes the old traditional pattern[23] of describing plants and passes on the newer idea.

There is good reason that our attention is drawn to the fact that vegetation has power to reproduce itself. In a subtle style the author exposes the impotence of the fertility gods by revealing that God implanted the power of reproduction in vegetation itself. In other words, the bountiful and fruitful earth was not dependent on the deities of fertility.

When God commanded the soil to produce vegetation, it implied that the earth was very much alive. It was alive with rich organic life. Poetically speaking, earth responds obediently to God's word by sprouting plants and trees. In my poem Creation[24] I retell the appearance of the earth and vegetation as follows:

Sound was heard. The soil moved.
The ground heaved. The mountains peaked.
There was life! There was green!
Plants came out from hiding.
The earth groaned. The trees stood.
Movement was everywhere.

---

[23]Earlier creation accounts about vegetation describe plants as food for human consumption. But the author of Genesis describes the general divisions of plants according to their kind. Here we find traces of scientific thinking.

[24]See Chapter 4 for the complete poem.

CELESTIAL LUMINARIES
GENESIS 1:14-19

Then God exclaimed: Let there be lights in the firmament of the sky to separate the day from the night; and let them be for signs, and for seasons, and for days and for years! And let them shine in the firmament of the sky to give light on the earth! And that is how it happened. So God made two great lights, the larger light to rule over the day and the smaller light to rule over the night and the stars. And God entrusted them to the firmament of the sky to give light on the earth, and to rule over the day and over the night, and to separate the light from the darkness. And God saw that it was beautiful. Now it was evening, then it was morning, day four.

Note the similarity between verses 3 and 14. Gen. 1:3 says "Let there be light." Gen 1:14 says "Let there be lights." This section on the fourth day is considerably longer than the sections on the first three days. The author repetitiously and successively tells of the duties of the heavenly bodies and informs us of the reasons for their functions. The sun and moon are to function in four basic ways: 1) to separate, 2) to indicate, 3) to give light, 4) to rule. All these functions are repeated except function (2) — to indicate.

This fourth-day detailed account is very important because Canaanite and Mesopotamian people worshipped the sun and the moon as principal deities. Celestial bodies were star gods. Even light was a deity, or at the least a deity who manifested as the light. The deity was either the god of the dawn or the sun god. The reader will notice that the narrative carefully omitted calling the larger light "sun" and the smaller light "moon." It says, "So God made two great lights, the larger light to rule over the day and the smaller light to rule over the night." Since the sun and the moon were worshipped as deities, the author resourcefully exposed these heavenly bodies as merely basic elements of the universe. In other words, the sun and the moon were not gods, but just "two great lights."

If the reader will recall, God created light on the first day. This act of creation (Gen. 1:3) was to show that light was not a deity. It was not the sun god or the god of the dawn; it was a creation of God. *Elohim,* the creator, was responsible for the existence of light. Furthermore, on the fourth day He commanded these heavenly bodies to appear so that they might help the light He had created on the first day.

In the Hebrew creation account, light, sun, moon, and stars were stripped of their divinity. It was no longer necessary to fear or worship any of these natural cosmic forces. Ancient peoples ritualized these nature elements in their worship. They did this to elicit their blessings. They also made sacrifices to these divinities to appease them and to allay their wrath toward humans.

Some scholars have suggested that verses 16 and 17 (named "action account") belong to an older stage of tradition. Verses 14 and 15 do not say anything about the lights ruling day and night and so forth as do verses 16 and 17. In the newer tradition (verses 14 and 15), it says, "Let there be lights in the firmament of the sky to separate the day from the night; and let them be for signs, and for seasons, and for days and for years." (Let the reader notice that the verb "to rule" is not present.) These verses specify the functions of the bodies of light: let them be for signs, seasons, days and years. The narrator describes the duties of the sun, moon, and stars in terms of the calendar.[25]

Before concluding this section of the narrative, one other point needs mentioning. Verse 14 says, " . . . and let them be for signs, and for seasons, and for days and for years!" There is some uncertainty over the interpretation "for signs and for seasons, . . . " Does it mean the lights are to serve "as signs for set times—the days and the years"? Or does it mean for "fixed times" such as new moons, festivals, and so forth? No one can determine which meaning the author intended.

LIFE IN ANIMATION
WATER AND SKY CREATURES
GENESIS 1:20-23

Then God exclaimed: Let the waters be teeming with swarms of living creatures and let the flying creatures fly above the earth and in the open expanse of the sky! So God created huge dragons and all living creatures that swarm which the waters brought forth according to their kind and every flying creature according to its kind. Now God saw that it was beautiful. Then God blessed them and said to them: Be fruitful and increase and fill the waters of the seas, and let the flying creatures increase on the earth! Now it was evening, then it was morning, day five.

---

[25]For a comparison of the Babylonian account of the stars and the biblical account, see Claus Westermann, *Genesis 1-11, a Commentary*, pp. 132–34.

This section of the narrative introduces something new, i.e., the blessing. The creation of sentient beings is a completely different form of creation. Thus the literary pattern changes to fit the new element of blessing. God speaks the creative word and He speaks the word of blessing.

God willed, and the waters filled with life in motion. The command does not say that the water is to generate swarms of living creatures. It merely says that the creatures of the water are to be present in the sea. Movement and life are the idea of the sea creatures.

"Winged creatures" or "flying creatures" also represent life in movement. The narrator groups the water creatures and the flying creatures in the same creative process. However, he does not tell us the full creative process.

SEA MONSTERS

"So God created huge dragons." The Aramaic word *taneeneh* and the Hebrew word *tanneeneem* mean "dragons," ("sea-dragons") "serpents," "whales," "crocodiles," "hippopotami," and "sea monsters." Early in Israel's history *taneen* was the mythical monster of Chaos. Later the term became a general reference for huge sea creatures. It also refers to the northern constellation Draco, part of which forms a semicircle around the Little Dipper.

Again, the Torah writer of creation makes a simple statement. *Tanneeneem,* (dragons or sea monsters)[26] are nothing more than huge water animals — sea creatures. They

---

[26]The Hebrew term *taneen* is the name of a primeval dragon-god that appears in the Canaanite myths from Ugarit.

are no longer divinities. Hebrew, Egyptian, Canaanite, and Mesopotamian legends refer to different primeval gods or monsters: the Dragon, Leviathan, Behemoth, the Flying Serpent, the Twisting Serpent, the Crooked Serpent, and many other monsters. However, in various passages of scripture they are nothing more than prosaic comparisons of evil.[27] Biblical sages and prophets also refer poetically to these sea monsters.

When God commanded the waters to produce swarms of living creatures, a poetic implication is signified. The same is true when God commanded the appearance of flying creatures. The waters fill with swarms of living creatures. And immediately following this event the sky fills with flying creatures. Although we refer to this chapter in Genesis as a narrative, we must remember that it is a prose poem. For a second time I refer to part of the poem Creation:[28]

Life was felt.
The air was turbulent. Flight was in motion.
The waters were disturbed. The sea was crowded.
Images were seen. The forms were dense.
Earth felt their weight!

The act of blessing goes hand in hand with sentient beings. Blessing in this passage emphasizes fertility and increase. Thus fruitfulness, increase, and filling the earth point to abundance. Blessings, in essence, translate as plenty, i.e., no lack. "Blessing implies creation and is effective as the work of the creator. To speak of life and its dynamism is to speak of

---

[27]Job 7:12, 40:15, 41:1; Isa. 27:1, 51:9–10; Ps. 74:13–14.
[28]See p. 15, footnote 20.

111

the effective action of the creator."[29] God's blessing closes the fifth day.

CREATURES OF THE EARTH
GENESIS 1:24-25

Then God exclaimed: Let the earth bring forth living creatures according to their nature: animals and reptiles and wild land beasts according to their nature! And that is how it happened. So God made the wild land beasts according to their nature and the animals according to their nature and all the reptiles of the earth according to their nature. And God saw that it was beautiful.

The sixth day corresponds to the third day, which is the appearance of dry land. "Let the earth bring forth living creatures" is different from "let the earth sprout vegetation." In the vegetation sequence the earth participates with its greening. In the creation of land animals, the expression means that the animals belong to the earth. The same idea of creation expressed in the fifth day is also present in the sixth day except that the pronounced blessing is missing. Biblical experts believe that the author deliberately recorded only three blessings.

We deeply respect the mountains, the fields, the trees, the ground beneath our feet. We also feel their vibrating energies and participate with them in the song of nature. And we breathe the life-sustaining oxygen they provide. But life in animated form is more precious to us than any other form. Animated forms such as fish, winged creatures of the sky, land

---

[29]Claus Westermann, *Genesis 1-11, a Commentary*, p. 140.

animals both wild and tame, and the small crawling ones vibrate and emit a kinship with us. The writer has a profound respect for the world of nature. He assigns the living creatures their right to exist and their proper place in creation. He calls upon us to respect their dignity as fellow creatures. God has created them.

The animal world shares with human beings the blessing of God. "Then God blessed them and said to them, Be fruitful and increase. . . ." Inanimate creations of God did not receive this special blessing. Higher forms of life are chosen for something more, and in this they join with humankind. Fish, winged creatures, and land animals are especially endowed by God in a way that is distinct from all other forms of creation. In a unique way they relate to divine power in that they create new life. God pronounced everything He had made as beautiful, but animals are *blessed* and beautiful.

In the creation narrative God had charged the water with life. Therefore it began to teem with swarms of living forms. Then He commanded the winged creatures to fly throughout the openness of the sky. The sensitive earth began to feel the weight and presence of the legged forms that traversed its surface. God filled His sanctuary, earth, with respiring, animated life. The author set the stage. Everything was in readiness to receive and support the presence of the human family.

PRAYER OF THE IROQUOIS

These acts of creation recall to mind a famous prayer from one of our Native American tribes:

113

THE PRAYER

We return thanks to the earth, who lives in us.
We return thanks to the waters, who flow in us.
We return thanks to the herbs, who heal us.
We return thanks to corn and bean and squash, who feed us.
We return thanks to bush and tree, who give us fruit.
We return thanks to wind, who banishes disease.
We return thanks to the moon and stars,
who give us light when the sky is dark.
We return thanks to the clouds, who give us rain.
We return thanks to the sun, who looks upon the earth
with a beneficent eye.
We return thanks to the Great Spirit, who blesses all things
for the good of his children.

Chapter 6

THE APEX OF CREATION

THE CREATION OF HUMAN BEINGS
GENESIS 1:26–27

Then God exclaimed: Let us make humankind in our image, as our resemblance! And they shall rule over the fish of the sea and over the flying creatures of the sky and over the animals and over the wild land beasts and over all the reptiles that creep on the earth! So God created humankind in his image in the image of God he created him, male and female, he created them.

A BENEFIT OR A TRAUMA?

This well-known biblical passage can be a great benefit or a trauma for Western society. It depends on how one interprets these verses. Some historians believe that this passage is the root of the Western world's exploitation of our environment and the abuse of our animal world.

The author seems to place humans in a highly exalted position by portraying them as God's image and likeness. Then he also grants them what might be interpreted as absolute control (dominion) over all the earth and its creatures. Do human beings have absolute power? Is this presentation of humankind grandiose?

Today there are some interpreters who believe humanity is the center of all things and that everything exists for the benefit of humankind. Was this the author's intent? Does the biblical writer see humanity as God's supreme creation? Let us examine this passage very carefully so that we may answer the above questions.

A DIVERGENCE

These verses are distinctly unique and noticeably diverge from earlier writing in Genesis 1. First we must realize that the creation of humans was at one time an independent narrative. It later became part of the story of the world's creation. This is the reason for its length and detail as told in the second half of the sixth day.[1]

Second, according to these verses, God does not create by His word. Instead, He involves Himself directly with the creation of humankind. The usual perfunctory phrase "Let there be . . ." changes into the intimate locution "Let us make . . . " Besides this divergence, the repetitive expression that frames each day, "God saw that it was beautiful," does not appear. However, slightly altered, it does surface in verse 31, where "everything" that God created is "exceedingly beautiful." The all-inclusive term "everything" refers to the creative works of all six days and not just to the animals and humans.

---

[1]The verses include 26–30. However, the entire creation of humans narrative is 26–29. Verse 30 includes the same provision made for both humans and animals.

TO WHOM WAS GOD SPEAKING?

Before continuing, there is a question I need to address. Wherever I have lectured in the United States and Canada, a specific biblical question consistently arises. That question is: "To whom was God speaking when He said 'Let **us** make man in **our** image, as **our** likeness'?" Since no one was there to see God creating, we realize that it is the author who is responsible for this saying. So why did the author have God speak in the plural form?

Several interpretations exist. In the early centuries of Christianity, the Church interpreted this phrase as the first hint of the Trinity: God the Father; God the son; God the Holy Ghost. This idea is extremely doubtful. The Church doctrine of the Trinity was not fully formulated or established until 325 C.E. When the Genesis creation account appeared, monotheism was at its peak. In fact, the prophets, during the monarchical period, were moving Israel into a radical form of monotheism. Thus the Semitic writer would never portray, or even hint that God was a trinity of persons. Neither would he suggest a triune nature.

OTHER INTERPRETATIONS

Another interpretation has it that the plural form refers to God and His heavenly court, i.e., an angelic host.[2] Other commentators think that this phrase echoes earlier non-Israelite

---

[2]Several scriptural passages describe the heavenly court: 1 Kings 22:19–22; Job 1:6; 2:1; 38:7; Ps. 89:6–7. Some scholars think that there is a parallel between Gen. 1:26 and Isa. 6:8.

legends. These legends tell us that the decision to create human beings took place in the council of the gods. However, both interpretations are unlikely since the narrator says nothing about God creating angels or any other supernatural beings (deities). His main theme is that God alone created the entire world. This being the case, God could not address or consult with any supernatural host, i.e., gods or angels. For the author, *elohim* is unique and supreme. Heaven contains no intermediary host or hierarchy. Only "winged creatures" occupy the sky.

For a very long time biblical interpreters thought that "Let us make . . . " was a "majestic plural." Today most commentators have abandoned this explanation entirely. Nevertheless, the key that unlocks the difficulty is the Semitic "let us" grammatical construction.[3]

PLURAL OF DELIBERATION

"Let us" is not the construction of a "majestic plural." It is "the plural of deliberation." Umberto Cassuto refers to this idea and calls it "the plural of exhortation." He says: "When a person exhorts himself to do a given task he uses the plural: 'Let us go!' 'Let us rise up!' 'Let us sit!' and the like."[4]

This style of speech occurs in self-deliberation. In 2 Sam. 24:14 we find a good example: "*Let us fall* into the hand of the LORD . . . but into the hand of man *let me not fall*."

---

[3]Hebrew grammarians call it a "cohortative." The consonant *noon* ("n") replaces the consonant *aleph* (silent letter) and is in accord with the linguistic rules of Palestinian Aramaic, meaning "Let."

[4]U. Cassuto, *A Commentary on the Book of Genesis: Part One, From Adam to Noah*, pp. 55–56.

The grammatical cohortative begins with the plural but ends with the singular.

Another example is Gen. 11:7–8. God says: "*Let us* go down . . . so *yahweh* scattered them." Again, it begins with a plural and ends with the singular — *yahweh*. According to most grammarians, the plural of deliberation in the cohortative is well attested and explains the author's grammatical application.

Genesis 1 clearly tells us that the creation of humanity was a divine decision. This idea, the divine decision, was also a common Near Eastern creation motif. The biblical author passes on what has been known among all Near Eastern peoples.

GOD'S IMAGE

"Then God exclaimed: Let us make humankind in our image, as our resemblance! And they shall rule. . . ." This verse recalls to mind the questions that arose at the beginning of this chapter: "Is the author's appraisal of humankind grandiose?" "Was he ascribing absolute power to human beings?" The simple answer to both questions is of course that he was not.

Let us look at another verse: "Then *yahweh* God formed the human from the dust of the ground, and he blew into his nostrils the breath of life and the human became a living being."[5] The emphasis of scripture here is upon humankind's fragility and vulnerability. After all, human beings are made from the "dust of the ground." The author does not present a grandiose appraisal of humanity. God's image does not express

---

[5]Gen. 2:7, Aramaic Peshitta Text, Errico translation.

a special lordship or divine sovereignty for humankind, but something much more simple.

Explicitly and passionately the inspired poet sees humanity in a unique position and relationship to the transcendental — *elohim* God. There is no grandiosity here as one might suppose. It is a highly dignified declaration of the value of a human being, especially in relation to the creator. It is true that humans are akin to animals and are extremely vulnerable and excessive in injurious behavior. Nonetheless, the creation writer is fully aware of the total capacity of a human being.

A CHIP OFF THE OLD BLOCK

A group of biblical teachers once asked me what I thought the Hebrew/Aramaic expression "in our image and our likeness" meant. Before I could answer, one of them began reciting a long list of possible meanings that he thought would apply. Before he could finish, I interrupted him and said: "If I were to paraphrase this verse and attempt to interpret its meaning from a simple point of view, I would translate it this way: 'Then God exclaimed, let's make a chip off the old block'." The scholar was taken aback by the expression "chip off the old block." He was shocked at its simplicity. But that is precisely its meaning! God created humanity in His image and likeness so that He might commune with His creation, just as caring parents commune with their children. In other words, "image and likeness" reveals the potential for interaction between God and the human family.

A HUMAN ILLUSTRATION

Furthermore, we must realize that the terms "image" and "likeness" are illustrations. That is, they are abstract. Any attempt to perceive them literally is to misconstrue their simplicity. My freewheeling translation of Gen. 1:26 as "a chip off the old block" clearly illustrates this point.

The basic difficulty here is that the actual creation of humankind is hidden from us. We do not know how God created the human family, nor does the author. The narrator simply says God created humankind in His image and resemblance.

God is imageless, intangible, and invisible. How can one describe the unknown? The best one can do is describe the unknown with the known. A human being is the tangible, visible image of God. This does not imply that God is a corporeal being. The "image and likeness" idea was not meant to be scrutinized but understood in a simple manner: God and a human being can commune.

ONE TRANSCENDENTAL SOURCE

Humanity, as God's image, signifies one transcendental source for all races and supersedes any notion of ethnic hierarchy. Hebrew sages clearly understood that this passage was intended to encourage social harmony among races. According to this text, no one race or individual can claim a unique ancestry as a pretext for asserting superiority over other members of the human family.

In the Mishnah[6] we read: "Man was created single for the sake of peace among men so that no one might say to his fellow: My father was greater than yours." And, in another Jewish writing it says: "Beloved is man for he was created in the image of God. Still greater was God's love in that He gave to man the knowledge of his having been so created."[7]

CORPOREAL OR SPIRITUAL IMAGE?

The word for "image" in Aramaic is *zlma*. It is related to the Akkadian *zalmu,* which had the double meaning of "image" and "statue." *Zlm* is its Semitic root. This term applied precisely to idols that were cast in human form and considered divine. The Aramaic term *zlma* also signifies "statue" and "idol." The word *dmutha*, "likeness" in Aramaic and Hebrew, also means "resemblance," or "look-alike."

Originally in all other Near Eastern texts "image and likeness" pointed to a corporeal resemblance. However this is not the emphasis of the Hebrew narrator. Nor does he describe a spiritual resemblance. The author emphasizes the connection between God and the human family.

All other creations of God (light, seas, sun, moon, stars, etc.) represent His handiwork. God's handiwork cannot commune with Him. They are the wonders and marvels of His creative expression. On the other hand, humanity not only is a creation of God, but as His image may communicate with the creator. This is the critical and essential difference between all creative acts of God and the creation of humankind.

---

[6]A Hebrew legal codification containing the core of the moral law.
[7]*Ethics of the Fathers* 3:18.

I reiterate that the writer stated his case very succinctly when he wrote that humankind was God's image. Just as our children are our image and likeness, so humanity is, figuratively speaking, God's created offspring. In other words, humanity was created for communion with God. Each human being as a creation of God is unique. "Every man should know that since creation no other man ever was like him. Had there been such another, there would be no need for him to be. Each is called on to perfect his unique qualities."[8]

SCHOLARLY CONCLUSIONS

According to the Jewish scholar Umberto Cassuto, the word "image" in the creation text antedates any literal corporeal significance.[9] But he does interpret the word "image" on a spiritual level. However, many other scholars claim that the narrator's use of the term "image" refers to the whole person. They hold that the author does not divide humanity into spiritual and corporeal classifications. In fact, Hebrew scripture makes no separation between the spiritual and the corporeal.[10] Despite these scholarly conclusions, we must remember that "image and likeness" is an abstract idea and not a literal one. The prime thought of "image and likeness" characterizes the

---

[8]Baal Shem Tov. Buber, *Die chassiduschen Bucher* (Berlin: Schocken, 1927) tr. W. Gunter Plaut p. 157.

[9]See Umberto Cassuto, *A Commentary on the Book of Genesis, Part One, From Adam to Noah*, p. 56.

[10]See Claus Westermann, *Genesis 1–11: A Commentary*, p. 150, (4.). Also, for a full discussion concerning the word "image," see Westermann's Excursus: "The History of the Exegesis of Gen. 1:26-27," pp. 147–55.

medium through which interaction between God and a human being takes place.

THE ENIGMA

As an aside, I would like to address a question that is often asked during my lectures on creation. "If human beings are created in the image of God, why are we prone to failure and hopelessness?" In response I usually say: "The human condition is an enigma. For you see, in our essence we are spirit, and in our expression we are human. To put it another way, we are divinely human and humanly divine."

As human beings we can soar to great heights and fall to extreme depths. Through choice, we may either terrorize or tranquilize ourselves. We are born sensitive and strong. Yet we are vulnerable. We possess astounding potential for anything we wish to be or do. However, we also possess a potential to err. It is unfortunate that fallibility is often equated with failure and evil. The thought of fallibility does not mean that we are, in essence, failures. Nor is it valid to equate fallibility with evil.

Modern thinking has enthroned two opposing gods: the god of success and the god of failure. These gods have supplanted God and the devil. We worship the god of success and sacrifice ourselves, our families, our energies, and our time to him as we flee from the clutches of the horrific god of failure.

In our culture, pressure is upon us to achieve meritorious and outstanding goals, to be winners, to dress and to live successfully. It is apparent that no room is made for so-called flawed, fallible creatures. But let us recognize that fallibility does not spell out a flawed creature. It is a human characteristic that makes us vulnerable. Fallibility helps us realize humility. It also provides us with an opportunity to grow in compassion, understanding, and love for ourselves and for others. When fallibility is accepted and not resisted, then that very vulnerability creates a pathway of compassion where fear can no longer dominate our minds. When this idea is fully comprehended we become free to make mistakes without guilt, shame, or condemnation.

Again, when we truly understand ourselves as God's image, we learn to forgive and release ourselves from self-imposed oppression. Then we discover rich self-contentment. We come to realize that life does not compel us, but impels us; we are no longer driven, but guided.

The inherent "image" of God (our communion with God) is the fundamental ground of being. This "image" is not a guarantee of perfection. Rather, it is a state of companionship in which we are to realize our creator. It also becomes the fertile soil in which each individual's heart and mind is nurtured and nourished. The psalmist aptly and poetically describes humanity in the following song:

What is a human being
that You keep him in remembrance?
And the ordinary individual
that You have looked after him?
You have set him a little lower than the angels,
and have clothed him with splendor
and with magnificence.
And You have given him power
over the works of Your hands.
And You have put all things under his feet:

all sheep and oxen,
and the beasts of the wilds,
and the birds of the sky,
and the fishes of the sea which pass
through the paths of the seas. . . . [11]

Both the Hebrew writer of the Genesis creation narrative
and the poetical psalmist depict humanity very differently from
the Assyrio-Babylonian account, which says: "Blood I will mass
and cause bones to be. I will establish a savage, 'man' shall be
his name. Verily, savage man I will create. He shall be charged
with the service of the gods that they might be at ease!"[12] Is
not this description of the creation of man by the creator god
Marduk of Mesopotamia truly different from the affirmative
description of humankind by the God of Israel? According to
the biblical story, man is not a servant to put the gods at ease
but a creature that communes with his creator.

THE TERM ADAM

"So God created humankind in his image in the image of
God he created him, male and female he created them."[13] The
Semitic term *adam* is usually translated as "man," "human being"
or "humankind," irrespective of gender. In Aramaic *nasha*, as
well as *adam*, means "human being," or "humankind." The root
of the word signifies "red," "blood," "ruddy," or "ruby." And

---

[11]Ps. 8:4–8, Aramaic Peshitta Text, Errico translation.

[12]*Enuma Elish: The Creation Epic* in James B. Pritchard, *Ancient Near Eastern Texts*, pp. 60–72.

[13]Gen. 1:27, Aramaic Peshitta Text, Errico translation.

what is most interesting, the word for "ground" in Hebrew is *adamah*. This implies that "Adam" was of the red earth or ground.

Some commentators think that there is a strong biblical link between ancient belief in the magical forces of the red beds of earth and the Hebrew writer naming the original man *adam* — "red earthling," "groundling." Scientific research informs us that the red beds of earth are coated with iron oxides and that these oxides were formed from free oxygen. Furthermore, it has been determined that blue-green algae cells belong to the oldest known organisms. These cells produce from themselves the free oxygen upon which all life depends.

RED EARTH

In many primitive cultures red ocher was a symbol of life-giving substance. Ocher is any of the various natural earths that are used as pigments. They range in color from pale yellow to orange, brown, and red and consist of mixtures of hydrated oxides of iron with varying proportions of clay. The color red was the most significant color in the ancient world. Red was associated with divinity and related to temporal power among priests and royalty. It was also associated with evil. In primitive rituals red ocher was used to ward off evil, and that is how it also became connected with evil. The prophet Isaiah says: " . . . though your *sins* are like *scarlet*, . . . "

In present-day India, red ocher is used in cases of illness and at marriage ceremonies. Among certain African tribes when anyone becomes ill, the body is lathered and spread with this red clay. Apparently even today this very old belief in the healing and magical forces of the red earth persists.

There is also a popular etymology that connects the ancient Akkadian word *adamatu* with *adam,* or *admu* — "man." Later in history this name reappears in the Bible as the name of the first man. The term *adam* refers to "red skins" or a "reddish dark brown" color. Other commentators hold that the Akkadians, who were the first Semites in Iraq, were not Caucasian. They were of the dark race and known as "black-faces." However, "blackfaces" are not to be confused with the dark-skinned Ethiopians.

MALE AND FEMALE

The biblical writer understands that the "image" of God is both male and female. What, then, is humanity? Humanity is God's image and likeness, male and female. The biblical text does not teach a single-gender model of humanity. Neither should one imagine that the original human being was a singular anatomical bisexual. Some biblical commentators have interpreted the meaning of "Adam" in the Genesis story as a bisexual being.

According to Gen. 1:27, male and female form two distinct sexes. This is an important aspect of the Hebrew creation story. The terms "male and female" in the text refer to the genital distinction between the sexes. The idea that the first Adam was a bisexual being is not the thought of the creation author. This notion was a late interpretation stemming from rabbinic and Hellenistic schools of thought.

On the other hand, ancient Greek thought imagined a one-sex/one-flesh model.[14] And that perfect single-gender was the human male. Furthermore, it is incredible to think that this Greek idea held firmly from classical antiquity to the end of the seventeenth century. The Greeks believed that the female form was a sexual deformity of the one-sex male-model body.[15] Interestingly, misogyny also dominated Greek culture.

Biblical stories, including the creation narrative, transformed ancient myths of the gods and goddesses. As it did so, it introduced a change in thinking about nature, humanity, gender and culture. Without any doubt, the author of the creation narrative perceived male and female as complementary to each another. However, the Bible does not present us with well-developed male and female role models. It is further lacking in polemics concerning the dynamics of sexual energy. "There is a vacuum in an essential area of human concern. This vacuum [in the Bible] was ultimately filled (in Hellenistic times) by the complex of antiwoman, anticarnal ideas that had such a large impact on the development of Western religion and civilization."[16]

---

[14]"As a philosopher Aristotle insisted upon two sexes, male and female. But he also insisted that the distinguishing characteristic of maleness was immaterial and as a naturalist, *chipped away* at *organic distinctions between the sexes* so that what emerges in an account in which *one flesh* could be ranked, ordered, and distinguished as particular circumstances required." Thomas Laqueur, *Making Sex: Body and Gender from the Greeks to Freud*, p. 28.

[15]See Thomas Laqueur, *Making Sex: Body and Gender from the Greeks to Freud*, Chapter 2, "Destiny is Anatomy," pp. 25–34.

[16]Tikva Frymer-Kensky, *In the Wake of the Goddesses: Women, Culture and the Biblical Transformation of Pagan Myth*, chapter 17, "Sex and Gender," p. 198.

DOMINION

"And they [humankind] shall rule over the fish of the sea and over the flying creatures of the sky and over the animals and over the wild land beasts and over all the reptiles which creep on the earth!"[17] This portion of verse 26 has been and continues to be misunderstood. The author is not saying that humanity has absolute control or power over nature and the animal kingdom. He uses the stately language of great Mesopotamian empires to denote humanity's rulership (dominion) over animals. However, this dominion does not suggest a right to exploit nature.

The author clearly tells us that the human race is not inherently sovereign. It is God who delegates to the human family sovereignty over animals, and this sovereignty is to be exercised under God's grace and law. Furthermore, this delegated power to humanity is not absolute.

The Semitic author likens humanity's dominion to an Israelite monarch who was obliged to fulfill divine law while exercising kingly dominion and responsibility. The Israelite king was subject to accountability. Therefore, humanity's sovereignty is also limited. Humankind is accountable and responsible for the care of the environment. Although the human family rules over animals, according to verse 29, humanity may not consume them for food.[18] (Later in the biblical story humanity receives permission to consume animal flesh for food.)

When reading scripture, we seldom consider the context of biblical writings or the cultural background of the early Near

---

[17]Gen. 1:26b, Aramaic Peshitta Text, Errico translation.

[18]See verse 29, which limits humanity's diet to herbs, seeds, plants, vegetables, and fruits. But in Gen. 9:3–4 humankind could eat animal flesh.

East. For example, ancient religious beliefs concerning nature and the animal kingdom dominated the Near Eastern mind. The thinking was that nature, animals, the heavens, and their celestial bodies were divinities that ruled over humankind. In the creation story this idea is reversed. Nature and the animal world are now understood in their rightful place. They are not divinities. They are fellow-creatures sharing the world with humanity.

Primitive religious beliefs placed nature between the gods and humanity. But the Hebrew creation story places humankind between God and nature. Humans have dominion over nature. Thus a hierarchy of order is thereby established.

THE BLESSING
GENESIS 1:28

Then God blessed them and said to them: Be fruitful and increase and fill the earth and master it! And rule over the fish of the sea and over the flying creatures of the sky and over the wild land beasts and over all the animals that walk on the earth!

A DIRECT BLESSING

The reader will notice that the creation text reports God blessing and speaking directly to the man and woman whom He had just created. Here we have the transcendent creator God becoming the immanent God by speaking directly to His creation. This idea carries out the meaning of Genesis 1:26: "Let us make humankind in our image. . . ." God communes

131

with His image, the man and the woman. We must keep in mind that this is a primeval event and, as such, stands as a precedent for all time.

The blessing upon man and woman "to be fruitful and multiply and fill the earth" is typical of a Near Eastern father's blessing upon his sons and daughters. I visualize and hear Eastern parents looking at their son or daughter about to be married and saying to them: "Be fruitful and multiply." This is why these same words are attributed to God when He speaks to His "image and likeness."

There is an episode in Gen. 24:58–60 which illustrates, on a very human level, the typical eastern blessing of fertility. Rebecca's mother has just given her daughter permission to go with Abraham's servant to marry Isaac. She is to leave her home in Haran and find a new life with her husband in Palestine.

Rebecca's mother and Laban, her brother, along with their guests are present in the home. As her daughter is about to depart, Rebecca's mother and brother follow "the bride to be" to the door. Then, lifting their open palms while looking up towards heaven, they in very loud voices make affectionate petitions within the hearing of the multitudes of guests, who echo their words in chorus: . . "Be the mother of thousands and of millions, and let your descendants inherit the lands of their enemies. . . ."[19] "Thousands and millions" is certainly a blessing that multiplies the divine saying "be fruitful and multiply."

---

[19]For the complete and interesting story one needs to read Gen. 24:1–61.

MASTERING THE EARTH

Kabash, "to trample upon," is the Hebrew word translated as "subdue" in this verse. Too many interpreters take this word on face value only. But the term "master" the earth means "to subdue" — that is, "to work" — the ground. Therefore work or vocation in life was always to be a blessing and a part of human existence. Again, the words "subdue" or "master" do not refer to abuse, misuse, or exploitation of the earth. This verse does not provide us with a justification for exploiting our ecosystem. To do so is a complete distortion of the biblical truth, which prohibits such exploitation. Humankind does have dominion and can subdue (master) the earth, but only under the laws and grace of God. Humanity is accountable for its actions.

THE VEGETARIAN DIET
GENESIS 1:29–30

Then God said: Behold I have given you every herb-yielding seed that is planted upon the surface of the earth, and every tree that bears fruit-yielding seed; to you it shall be for food. And to every animal of the field and to all flying creatures of the sky and to everything that creeps on the earth that has life [I give] all tender green herbs for food. And that is how it happened.

These verses declare that not only human beings but also animals are included in the vegetarian world. These verses describe animals as herbivorous creatures. It is not until the

133

post-alluvion world that *yahweh* God grants humankind permission to consume animal flesh for food.[20]

THE CLOSE OF THE SIXTH DAY
GENESIS 1:31

Then God observed everything that He had made. And behold: It was exceedingly beautiful! Now it was evening, then it was morning, day six.

The reader will recall that the Hebrew word *tov* has three distinct connotations: An aesthetic quality, a moral quality, and "good," in the sense of function and purpose.[21] God declares the works of the six days to be exceedingly good and beautiful in appearance and function.

The creator made specific divisions and lines of demarcation not to be crossed. This orderliness holds back chaos. The Genesis narrative tells us that creation is now complete and in balance. This is the reason God declares everything "good."

The expression used continually throughout the Aramaic creation narrative, ". . . that it was beautiful," in this verse is augmented by the exclamation "It was exceedingly beautiful!" In the Hebrew text the phrase ". . . that it was good" also becomes amplified as "It was very good!"

We often lose sight of the goodness and orderliness of our earth and its environment. We feel it necessary to change and cross over forbidden borders, which has heaped painful consequences upon us. Humanity has opened the door on

---

[20]See Gen. 9:3–4.

[21]See Chapter 5, subheading "Good or Beautiful."

chaos. Because of this, the universe appears menacing, for, to be sure, chaos is always present behind balance and harmony.

> The Lord created the world in a state of beginning. The universe is always in an uncompleted state, in the form of its beginning. It is not like a vessel at which the master works to finish it; it requires continuous labor and renewal by creative forces. Should these cease for only a second, the universe would return to primeval chaos.[22]

The reader will recall that God did not destroy the darkness but stabilized it with light. However, let us not forget that chaos is persistent. Yet, in spite of its persistence, we acknowledge the basic goodness of creation. We, as custodians of the earth, remain responsible for our planet in alliance and compliance with the laws of God.

THE CONCLUDING IDEA

The flowing, rhythmic narrative finally draws to a close and the six days are complete. God, like a master artist, having finished His painting, makes a final survey: *And Alaha* [God] *saw everything that He had made, behold: exceedingly beautiful! And it came to be evening, and it came to be morning, the sixth day.*[23]

---

[22]R. Simchah Bunam, quoted by Louis I. Newman, *The Hasidic Anthology* (New York: Bloch, 1944), p. 61.

[23]A literal translation of Gen. 1:31, Aramaic Peshitta Text, Errico translation.

Chapter 7

GOD'S FINAL DAY

THE SEVENTH DAY
GENESIS 2:1-3

And they were finished, the heavens and the earth and all their powers. Now on the sixth day God had finished His works that He had made. So He rested on the seventh day from all His works that He had made. Then God blessed the seventh day and made it holy because on that day He rested from all His works that He had created and made.

The reader will recall that the order of creation is set in a literary pattern of seven days, known as the heptadic principle. Six creative days and one day of rest $(6+1=7)$[1] shaped the creation narrative. However, the seventh day (Gen. 2:1-3) is uniquely distinct from the six days that have preceded it.

Humanity is undoubtedly the pinnacle of the creation narrative. But the heart of the account is God as creator. It is His creative work. This final day belongs completely to Him. Creation begins with God and closes with God. The narration is not a historical account; it describes the primeval event of creation.

Gen. 2:1 recalls Gen. 1:1. Grammatically speaking, it opens with God as subject, the heavens and the earth as object. The creator made everything, including what was not expressly

---

[1]See Chapter 1, subheading "The Number Seven," and Chapter 5, subheading "The Literary Pattern."

mentioned in Chapter 1. Gen. 1:1 and 2:1 tell the complete story: God created the entire universe.

The Hebrew text says: "Thus the heavens and the earth were finished, and all the host of them." The term "host" has spawned varied interpretations. One interpretation says that "host" refers to angels. This explanation is misleading. "Host" (in Aramaic, "powers") indicates the sun, the moon, the stars, and all heavenly bodies. It is also used in relation to the earth and its many powers. The point is this: "host" is a figure of speech.

SIXTH DAY VERSUS SEVENTH DAY

Gen. 2:2 of the Aramaic Peshitta and Hebrew Masoretic texts differ. Aramaic says: "Now on the **sixth** day God had finished His works. . . ." The Masoretic text says: "And on the **seventh** day God finished the work. . . ." A difficulty arises in the Hebrew rendering of verse two, for God did not complete His work on the seventh day, but on the sixth.

The Aramaic text is not the only translation that uses the sixth day. Samaritan and Septuagint versions also read "sixth" instead of the "seventh." Did translators of these three versions deliberately make this change? Or did an original Hebrew text also read "sixth day"?

Scholars disagree on this issue. However, a strong preference exists in favor of the Hebrew rendering, "seventh day."[2] The Hebrew text plainly means that when the seventh day arrived God had already finished His work. In other words,

---

[2]See U. Cassuto, *A Commentary on the Book of Genesis: Part One, from Adam to Noah*, pp. 61–62.

by the seventh day the work had been completed. It is difficult for us to follow this line of thinking. Nonetheless, this is a Semitic style of writing.

THE DAY OF REST

Many people are amused with the idea of God resting from His labors. This stems from a literal reading of the text. God did not need respite from His creative works. The seventh day of cessation is a human description of a primordial event.

It is important to understand that the seventh day is a celebration of the creative activity now finished. The day of rest was a common motif among most primitive creation stories. Its significance is that the creator no longer intervenes with his completed works. Any intervention would be a disturbance within the natural order he has established.

Many translators render the Hebrew verb *wayyishboth*, "and He rested," as "and He ceased." Others translate it as "and He abstained." The Aramaic verb *wittneeh*, "and He rested," derives from the root *nwh* and means "to cease," "to soothe," "to assuage," "to satisfy."

THE HOLY DAY

Human beings are not the focal point of the creation account. It ends in the blessing and holiness of the seventh day. The narrative emphasizes God's sovereignty and the idea that He created the earth in which we live. Human beings do not own the earth, because they did not bring it into existence.

The blessing that appears in Gen. 2:3, "Then God blessed the seventh day and made it holy . . . " is unlike the blessings described in Gen. 1:22 and 28. This blessing is directed at time itself. The seventh day becomes a day set apart and infused with a special vitality all its own. God through His creative works reveals His sovereignty over the spatial. Here the writer declares that God is sovereign over time by blessing it.

The Aramaic term *qadeesha* means "holy," "sanctified," "to consecrate," "to set apart," and "to refresh." It comes from the Semitic root *qdsh*, "apartness," "sacredness." One can easily see that humanity imitates the divine pattern. We usually set aside one day (be it Saturday, Sunday, or any day) each week to rest and refresh ourselves. This designation is a subtle celebration of the sacredness of existence.

A REVIEW OF THE CREATION EPIC

I think the author of Gen. 1:1–2:3 did not intend this writing to be the last word on creation. We now know much of the history behind this composition. The narrator is both receiver and giver of ancient Near Eastern stories and folklore. He was immersed in a milieu of traditions and passed them on. He unquestionably reworked some of them. And to some extent, he presents us with original material on creation. Before this epic became part of the biblical canon, there were many other Israelite and non-Israelite stories of creation. Clearly, our narrator was not the first one to compose a poem about creation.

The author did not think in the scientific and theological terminologies of our world. Neither could he realize that his writings would create such a rift between science and religion

140

as exists today. Although the writing is timeless, he plainly wrote for his day and time.

The narrator stripped heaven and earth of their ancient divinities. He opened them to human research and placed an awesome responsibility upon the shoulders of the human family. Divine beings no longer stood between humankind and nature as explanations for the universe and its powers. Humans could now choose to explore, discover, and explain their world without these mysterious divinities.

MONOTHEISM AND POLYTHEISM

The monotheistic creation epic, in contrast to polytheistic creation depictions, generated and stimulated for humanity new forms of rational thinking. According to Max Weber, we can be grateful for the insights of ancient biblical ideas because they helped form the roots of Western rationalism.[3]

In polytheism the gods are not sovereign. They are usually controlled by a higher order, a supradivine impersonal force. In monotheism, God as creator reigns supreme and is both transpersonal and personal. *Elohim* acts transpersonally by no longer interfering with nature — Gen. 2:2. On the other hand, *elohim* acts personally by speaking directly to His "image and likeness," i.e., humankind — Gen. 1:26-28.

In earlier chapters I said that creation was a mystery. The author of Gen. 1:1-2:3 does not explain creation. He keeps it a holy mystery. He exalts and praises the majesty of God as creator through His magnificent creative works. And he

---

[3]Max Weber, *The Religion of China*, trans. and ed. by Hans H. Gerth.

narrates and teaches a reverence for the inaccessible mystery of creation and life.

Our sciences, which are human attempts to describe primordial events, cannot explain the fullness of the universe or the wonder of the appearance of humankind. The universe and the planet in which we live are incomprehensible, inscrutable, and indescribable. Therefore the heart and secret of our universe are kept from us.

Genesis 1 does not tell us to have faith in God. Rather, it tells a story that belongs to the entire human family. The author uses the generic term for deity, *elohim*. He gives no specific name for God. Although an Israelite, he does not imbue the narrative with the name of his national deity, *yahweh*. However, subsequent biblical authors do connect the trans-personal creator God in Genesis 1 with their national god — *yahweh*. Here the author deliberately omitted the specific name of God. His story embraced all of humanity and not just the nation Israel. In the narrative he emphasized the universality of the creator and humankind.

HUMAN RESPONSIBILITY

Genesis 1 introduces to humankind its responsibility to the earth and its environment. According to Scripture, the parameters of our existence are and always have been the earth. What we do or don't do with our environment and ourselves always returns to us. Scripture tells us that our destiny is the earth, not heaven. We are foremost humans,[4] that is, earthy creatures with a spiritual dimension to our being.

The creation account reports that God empowered humankind to fulfill its commitment to the world. The joys and agonies that we create here on earth are our responsibility. According to the narrative, all things function with meaning and purpose. This is why Scripture says, "it is exceedingly good."

Will we recognize our destiny? Will we exercise our right to improve social world order so that we, with God, can say, "It is exceedingly good"? Today one of the most powerful and destructive forms of chaos,[5] that is rampant in our world is violence. Who is responsible for this?

Human beings alone are responsible for violence and chaos on all levels. What is our dominion to be? A reign of terror? Or, a peaceful coexistence with each other, the animal world, nature, and the earth? We are empowered to convert our energies of violence into constructive energies. *"Man truly becomes human as he attempts to do godly deeds."*[6]

SUMMARY

This is what the biblical narrative tells us: We have dominion under the universal laws of God to create a better

---

[4]The word *human* stems from a theoretical Indo-European root *ghum* ("earth," "ground") from which the Latin *humus* "topsoil" or "earth" and the Old English *guma* ("man") are derived.

[5]Chaos in itself is not an evil. Order and boundaries keep chaos in balance. But when chaos reigns supreme, it destroys life as we know it. Let us recall that at one time the earth was chaos, which signifies that it did not have, nor could it support, a meaningful existence.

[6]W. Gunther Plaut, *The Torah: Genesis*, p. 11.

society. Each individual is responsible to perceive the duality of light and chaos within his/her self. This inner act of perception will not destroy us. Surely, it will bring us into balance and enable us to change our world.

Chaos or goodness expressed in the world is only a reflection of our inner selves. The desire for peace within ourselves also works to bring about peace in our world. Desire is the motivation for action. The Hebrew cosmological depiction of a God-created "good" world in the biblical story is the ultimate purpose and destiny for the human family.

BIBLIOGRAPHY

Alter, Michael J. *What is the Purpose of Creation? A Jewish Anthology*. Northvale N.J.: Jason Aronson Inc., 1991.

Aviezer, Nathan. *In the Beginning: Biblical Creation and Science*. Hoboken, N.J.: KATV Pub. House, Inc., 1990.

Batto, Bernard F. *Slaying the Dragon: Mythmaking in the Biblical Tradition*. Louisville, Ky.: Westminster/John Knox Press, 1992.

Berlin, Adele. *The Dynamics of Biblical Parallelism*. Bloomington, Ind.: Indiana Univ. Press, 1985.

Blenkinsopp, Joseph. *The Pentateuch: An Introduction to the First Books of the Bible*. New York: Doubleday, 1992.

Carus, Paul. *The History of the Devil and the Idea of the Devil*. LaSalle, Il.: Open Court Pub. Co., 1900.

Cassuto, Umberto. *A Commentary on the Book of Genesis, Part One: From Adam to Noah*. Translated by Israel Abrahams. Jerusalem: Magnes Press, 1989.
_____. *The Documentary Hypothesis: Eight Lectures*. Translated by Israel Abrahams. Jerusalem: Magnes Press, 1983.

Davies, Paul. *God and the New Physics*. New York: Simon & Schuster, 1983.
_____. *The Mind of God: The Scientific Basis for a Rational World*. New York: Simon & Schuster, 1992.

Errico, Rocco A. *The Message of Matthew: An Annotated Parallel Aramaic-English Gospel of Matthew.* Irvine, Calif.: Noohra Pub. 1991.

Forrester-Brown, James S. *The Two Creation Stories in Genesis: A Study of their Symbolism.* Berkeley, Calif.: Shambhala, 1974.

Fox, Everett. *In the Beginning: A New English Rendition of the Book of Genesis.* New York: Schocken Books, 1983.

Freedman, David Noel, Editor-in-Chief. *Anchor Bible Dictionary,* New York: Doubleday, 1992.
_____. *The Unity of the Hebrew Bible.* Ann Arbor, Mich. Univ. of Michigan Press, 1991.

Frymer-Kensky, Tikva. *In the Wake of the Goddesses: Women, Culture and the Biblical Transformation of Pagan Myth.* New York: The Free Press, 1992.

Graves, Robert and Patai, Raphael. *Hebrew Myths: The Book of Genesis.* New York: McGraw-Hill Books, 1966.

Heisenberg, Werner. *Physics and Beyond.* New York: Harper & Row, 1971.
_____. *Physics & Philosophy: The Revolution in Modern Science.* New York: Harper & Row, 1962.

Heschel, Abraham Joshua. *Man is Not Alone: A Philosophy of Religion.* New York: Noonday Press, 1990.

Holmes, Ernest S. *Your Invisible Power.* Los Angeles, Calif.: Science of Mind Publications, 1974.

Keightley, Alan. *Into Every Life a Little Zen Must Fall: A Christian Looks to Alan Watts and the East*. London: Wisdom Pub., 1986.

Knight, Douglas A. and Tucker, Gene M., Editors. *The Hebrew Bible and Its Modern Interpreters*. Chico, Calif.: Scholars Press, 1985.

Laqueur, Thomas. *Making Sex: Body and Gender from the Greeks to Freud*. Cambridge, Mass.: Harvard Univ. Press, 1990.

Larue, Gerald A. *Ancient Myth and Modern Life*. Long Beach, Calif.: Centerline Press, 1988.

Levenson, Jon D. *Creation and the Persistence of Evil: The Jewish Drama of Divine Omnipotence*. San Francisco, Calif.: Harper & Row, 1988.
_____. *Sinai and Zion: An Entry into the Jewish Bible*. San Francisco, CA: Harper & Row, 1985.

Halpern, Baruch and Levenson, John D., Editors. *Traditions in Transformation: Turning Points in Biblical Faith*. Winona Lake, IN: Eisenbrauns, 1981.

Hitti, Philip K. *The Near East in History: A 5000 Year Story*. Princeton: D. Van Nostrand Co., 1961.

Lamsa, George M. *Old Testament Light: A Scriptural Commentary Based on the Aramaic of the Ancient Peshitta Text*. Englewood Cliffs, N.J.: Prentice-Hall, 1964.

Mendel, Arthur P. *Vision and Violence*. Ann Arbor, Mich.: Univ. of Michigan Press, 1992.

Mettinger, Tryggve, N.D. *In Search of God: The Meaning and Message of the Everlasting Names*. Translated by Frederick H. Cryer. Philadelphia: Fortress Press, 1988.

Niditch, Susan. *Chaos to Cosmos: Studies in Biblical Patterns of Creation*. Chico, Calif.: Scholars Press, 1985.

O'Brien, Joan and Major, Wilfred. *In The Beginning: Creation Myths from Ancient Mesopotamia, Israel and Greece*. Chico, Calif.: Scholars Press, 1982.

O'Connor, M.P. *Hebrew Verse Structure*. Winona Lake, Ind.: Eisenbrauns, 1980.

Oden, Robert A., Jr. *The Bible without Theology: The Theological Tradition and Alternatives to It*. San Francisco: Harper & Row, 1987.

Plaut, W. Gunther. *The Torah: Genesis, A Modern Commentary*. New York: Jewish Pub. Society, 1974.

Pritchard, James B. *Ancient Near Eastern Texts: Relating to the Old Testament,* 2nd ed. with supplement. Princeton: Univ. Press., 1978

Radday, Yehuda and Shore, Haim. *Genesis: An Authorship Study*. Rome: Biblical Inst. Press, 1985.

Rihbany, A.M. *The Syrian Christ*. Boston: Houghton-Mifflin Co., 1916.

Sarna, Nahum M. *Genesis: The JPS Torah Commentary*. New York: Jewish Pub. Society, 1989.

Smith, Mark S. *The Early History of God: Yahweh and the Other Deities in Ancient Israel*. New York: Harper-Collins, 1990.

Speiser, E.A. *Genesis: A New Translation with Introduction and Commentary*. Garden City, N.Y.: Doubleday, 1964.

Sternberg, Meir. *The Poetics of Biblical Narrative: Ideological Literature and the Drama of Reading*. Bloomington, Ind.: Indiana Univ. Press, 1985.

Trible, Phyllis. *God and the Rhetoric of Sexuality*. Philadelphia: Fortress Press, 1978.

Von Franz, Marie-Louise. *Creation Myths: Patterns of Creativity*. Dallas: Spring Pub. 1986.

Weber, Max. *The Religion of China*. Translated and edited by Hans H. Gerth. Glenco, IL.: Free Press, 1951.

Westermann, Claus. *Genesis 1–11: A Commentary*. Translated by John J. Schullion, S.J. Minneapolis: Agusburg Pub. House, 1990.

_____. *Genesis: An Introduction*. Translated by John J. Schullion, S.J. Minneapolis: Fortress Press, 1992.

Westman, Heinz. *The Structure of Biblical Myths: The Onto-genesis of the Psyche*. Dallas: Spring Pub., 1983.

Williams, James G. *The Bible, Violence and the Sacred: Liberation from the Myth of Sanctioned Violence*. San Francisco: Harper & Row, 1991.

Wolf, Fred Alan. *Taking the Quantum Leap: The New Physics for Nonscientists*. San Francisco: Harper & Row, 1981.

Zeitlan, Irving M. *Ancient Judaism*. Oxford: Polity Press, Basil Blackwell, 1984.

In addition to *The Mysteries of Creation*, the Noohra Foundation is pleased to offer the following books by Dr. Rocco A. Errico.

ARAMAIC NEW TESTAMENT SERIES, VOLUMES 1 – 7
(DR. GEORGE M. LAMSA, CO-AUTHOR)

Aramaic Light on the Gospel of Matthew	$29.95
Aramaic Light on the Gospels of Mark & Luke	$26.95
Aramaic Light on the Gospel of John	$26.95
Aramaic Light on the Acts of the Apostles	$21.95
Aramaic Light on Romans through 2 Corinthians	$24.95
Aramaic Light on Galatians through Hebrews	$24.95
Aramaic Light on James through Revelation	(available Fall 2006)

These inimitable commentaries illuminate difficult and puzzling passages in the New Testament and offer unparalleled insight into the character and behavior of Near Eastern Semites. Dr. Errico has edited, expanded and annotated Dr. Lamsa's previous commentaries and added unpublished material that the two of them had drafted before Dr. Lamsa's death in 1975. Dr. Errico completed the comments they had outlined, adding information derived from his continual research in Aramaic word meanings and Near Eastern Semitic Studies.

LET THERE BE LIGHT

This illuminating work builds a bridge between Western ways of understanding and Near Eastern social realities in the Bible, helping us to see the Bible through Semitic, Aramaic eyes. It bypasses doctrinal creeds and rigid interpretations and corrects numerous errors and misleading literal translations that have caused confusion for centuries. This book provides seven key insights to understand the allusions, parables, and teachings of the Bible, opening the door to the ancient Aramaic world from which the Bible emerged. $17.95

AND THERE WAS LIGHT

As with *Let There Be Light*, this book takes us through the heart of the Hebrew Bible and New Testament by working with Aramaic and using the Seven Keys. Suddenly the Bible becomes clearer and more relevant for Western readers. The teaching ministry and parables of Jesus come alive as you've never read before. $19.95

SETTING A TRAP FOR GOD: The Aramaic Prayer of Jesus

What does the word "prayer" mean and what does it accomplish? Dr. Errico focuses on original Aramaic manuscripts and the ancient culture of the Near East as he answers these questions in his revised and expanded edition of the Lord's Prayer. Discover the way of peace, health, and prosperity as you learn to "set a trap" for the inexhaustible power of God. $10.95

THE MESSAGE OF MATTHEW: An Annotated Parallel Aramaic-English Gospel of Matthew

Dr. Errico's stirring translation of the ancient Aramaic Peshitta text of Matthew is further enriched with his stimulating and illuminating annotations. The English translation is printed on the left side of the page with footnotes. The Aramaic text is printed on the right with additional footnotes in English. These valuable footnotes explain the meanings of Aramaic words and customs with supplementary historical information. $24.95

CLASSICAL ARAMAIC: Book I

Learn to read and write the language of Jesus in a self-teachable format. Classical Aramaic is a practical grammar that prepares you to read the New Testament in Jesus' own native tongue. $24.95

LA ANTIGUA ORACIÓN ARAMEA DE JESÚS: El Padrenuestro

Dr. Errico's own translation into Spanish of his book *The Ancient Aramaic Prayer of Jesus*. $8.95

ACHT EINSTIMMUNGEN AUF GOTT: VATERUNSER

German translation and publication of *Setting a Trap for God*.

ES WERDE LICHT

German translation and publication of *Let There Be Light*.

OTTO ACCORDI CON DIO: IL PADRE NOSTRO ORIGINARIO

Italian translation and publication of *Setting a Trap for God*.

ABOUT THE AUTHOR
Rocco A. Errico

Dr. Rocco A. Errico is an ordained minister, international lecturer and author, spiritual counselor, and one of the nation's leading Biblical scholars working from the original Aramaic *Peshitta* texts. For ten years he studied intensively with Dr. George M. Lamsa, Th.D., (1890-1975), world-renowned Assyrian biblical scholar and translator of the *Holy Bible from the Ancient Eastern Text.* Dr. Errico is proficient in Aramaic and Hebrew exegesis, helping thousands of readers and seminar participants understand how the Semitic context of culture, language, idioms, symbolism, mystical style, psychology, and literary amplification—the *Seven Keys* that unlock the Bible—are essential to understanding this ancient spiritual document.

Dr. Errico is the recipient of numerous awards and academic degrees, including a Doctorate in Philosophy from the School of Christianity in Los Angeles; a Doctorate in Divinity from St. Ephrem's Institute in Sweden; and a Doctorate in Sacred Theology from the School of Christianity in Los Angeles. In 1993, the American Apostolic University College of Seminarians awarded him a Doctorate of Letters. He also holds a special title of Teacher, Prime Exegete, *Maplana d'miltha dalaha*, among the Federation of St. Thomas Christians of the order of Antioch. In 2002, Dr. Errico was inducted into the Morehouse College Collegium of Scholars.

Dr. Errico is a featured speaker at conferences, symposia, and seminars throughout the United States, Canada, Mexico and Europe and has been a regular contributor for over 24 years to *Science of Mind Magazine,* a monthly journal founded in 1927. He began his practice as an ordained minister and pastoral counselor in the mid-1950s and during the next three decades served in churches and missions in Missouri, Texas, Mexico, and California. Throughout his public work, Dr. Errico has stressed the nonsectarian, *open* interpretation of Biblical spirituality, prying it free from 2000 years of rigid orthodoxy, which, according to his research, is founded on incorrect translations of the original Aramaic texts.

In 1970, Dr. Errico established the Noohra Foundation in San Antonio, Texas, as a non-profit, non-sectarian spiritual-educational organization devoted to helping people of all faiths to understand the Near Eastern background and Aramaic interpretation of the Bible. In 1976, Dr. Errico relocated the Noohra Foundation in Irvine, California, where it flourished for the next 17 years. For seven years, the Noohra Foundation operated in Santa Fe, New Mexico, and in September 2001, it relocated to Smyrna, Georgia, where Dr. Errico is Dean of Biblical Studies for Dr. Barbara King's School of Ministry—Hillside Chapel and Truth Center.

Under the auspices of the Noohra Foundation, Dr. Errico continues to lecture for colleges, civic groups and churches of various denominations in the United States, Canada, Mexico and Europe.

———————

For a complimentary catalog of Aramaic Bible translations, books, audio and video cassettes, and a brochure of classes, retreats and seminars, or for any other inquiries, write or call the Noohra Foundation. Those interested in scheduling Dr. Errico for a personal appearance may also contact:

Noohra Foundation
PMB 343
4480 South Cobb Drive Ste H
Smyrna, GA 30080

Phone: 678-945-4006
Fax: 678-945-4966

Email: info@noohra.com
Noohra Foundation website: www.noohra.com